Crochet for Baby
All Year

Crochet for Baby
All Year
Easy-to-Make Outfits
for Every Month

TAMMY HILDEBRAND

STACKPOLE
BOOKS

Published by
STACKPOLE BOOKS
5067 Ritter Road
Mechanicsburg, PA 17055
www.stackpolebooks.com

Printed in the United States of America
10 9 8 7 6 5 4 3 2 1
First edition

Cover design by Tessa J. Sweigert

ISBN 978-0-8117-1324-5
Cataloging-in-Publication Data is on file with the Library of Congress.

Contents

Introductio

When I discovered that I was g
like any crocheter, my though
tiny outfits and blankets and bootie
later, we learned that we would be
made her appearance on December
gift for our family—and the inspirat

Each chapter presents an outfit (
version) with a theme specific to a r
rated at an easy skill level and work
to stitch them up quickly, as babies
aren't even babies anymore!

I hope you and your special littl
I enjoyed creating them!

CHAPTER ONE

January

New Beginnings

Begin the year and celebrate the beginning of a new life with a gorgeous christening gown. Made from a super-soft blend of baby alpaca, merino wool, and cashmere, this gown is sure to be an heirloom handed down from generation to generation.

Traditional Blessings Christening Gown

Even baby boys traditionally wear gowns for a christening ceremony. This simple and elegant gown will be the ideal choice if you are looking for a design that can be worn by all the boy and girl babies in the family.

SKILL LEVEL

EASY

YARN
Elann Collection Peruvian Baby Cashmere (60% Baby Alpaca, 30% Merino Wool, 10% Cashmere; 0.88 oz/25 g; 109 yd./100 m)
#0100 Parchment: 7 (8, 9) balls

CROCHET HOOK
U.S. size F-5 (3.75 mm) or size needed to obtain gauge

ADDITIONAL MATERIALS
3 buttons (shown: Blumenthal Lansing La Petite ⅝ in. [16 mm] Style #910 buttons)
3 yd. (2.75 m) ribbon, ⅛ in. (3 mm) wide
Yarn needle

SIZES
3–6 months (6–12 months, 12–18 months)
Note: Instructions are written for smallest size; changes for larger sizes are given in parentheses.

FINISHED MEASUREMENTS
Chest: 19½ (21, 22½) in. [49.5 (53.5, 57) cm]
Length: 28 (28, 28¾) in. [71 (71, 73) cm]

GAUGE
15 sc and 18 rows/rounds = 4 in. (10 cm)
4 lace pattern repeats = 4 in. (10 cm)
Note: One pattern repeat consists of [sc, ch 3, dc].
5 rounds in lace pattern = 3½ in. (9 cm)

SPECIAL STITCH
Foundation single crochet (fsc): *Step 1:* Place a slip knot on hook, ch 2, insert hook in 2nd ch from hook and draw up a loop; yarn over and draw through one loop on hook (the "chain"); yarn over and draw through 2 loops on hook (the "single crochet"). *Step 2:* Insert hook into the "chain" of the previous stitch and draw up a loop, yarn over and draw through one loop on hook (the "chain"), yarn over and draw through 2 loops on hook (the "single crochet"). Repeat for the length of foundation.

NOTES
The yoke is made first, working from the top down.

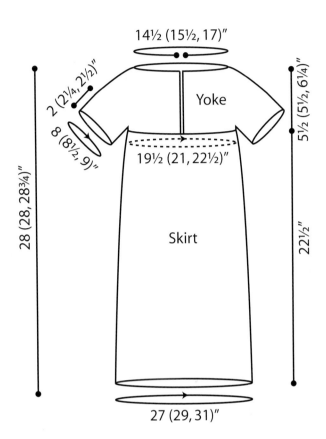

BOY

GOWN
Yoke
Fsc 54 (58, 64).
Row 1: Ch 1, turn, sc in first 9 (9, 10) sts (for front), 3 sc in next st, mark center st of 3 sc just made, sc in next 8 (9, 10) sts (for sleeve), 3 sc in next st, mark center st, sc in next 16 (18, 20) sts (for back), 3 sc in next st, mark center st, sc in next 8 (9, 10) sts (for sleeve), 3 sc in next st, mark center st, sc in last 9 (9, 10) sts (for front)—62 (66, 72) sc.
Rows 2–3: Ch 1, turn, sc in each st across.
Row 4: Ch 1, turn, [sc in each st to marked st, 3 sc in marked st] 4 times, sc in each st to end—70 (74, 80) sc.

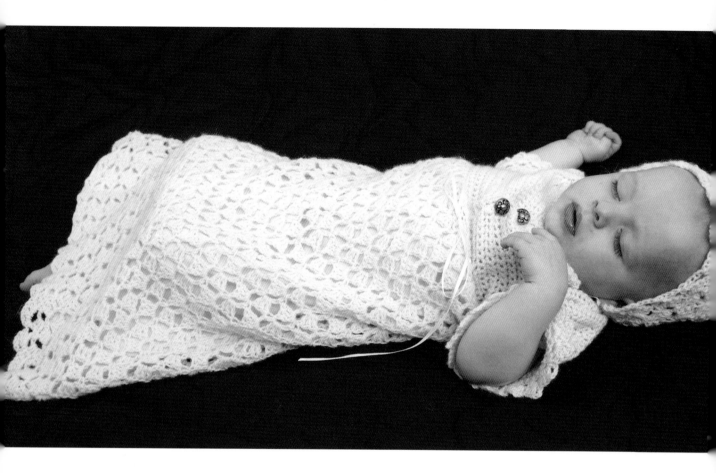

Rows 5–25 (25, 28): Repeat last 3 rows 7 (7, 8) times—
126 (130, 144) sc.

Sl st in first st of row 25 (25, 28) to join and begin working in rounds.

Divide for Sleeve Openings

Rnd 1: Ch 1, turn, sc in first 18 (18, 20) sts; ch 2 (3, 2),
sk next 28 (29, 32) sts (for sleeve opening), sc in next
34 (36, 40) sts, ch 2 (3, 2), sk next 28 (29, 32) sts (for
sleeve opening), sc in last 18 (18, 20) sts; join with sl
st in beg sc—70 (72, 80) sc and 2 underarm ch-sps.

Rnd 2: Ch 1, turn, sc in each st and ch around; join with
sl st in beg sc—74 (78, 84) sc.

Front Edging and Buttonhole Band

Row 1: With RS facing, join yarn with sl st around post
of st at end of row in top corner of left front to work
down left front edge; working around post of st at
end of each row, beginning in end of same row as
joining, [sc2tog, ch 1] 12 (12, 14) times, sc in end of
next 1 (1, 0) rows; working around post of st at end
of each row up right front edge, [sc2tog, ch 1] 12
(12, 13) times, end with sc in last row end for sizes
3–6 months and 6–12 months, sc2tog in last 2 row
ends for size 12–18 months.

NOTE When working row 2, work into each sc
and ch.

Row 2: Ch 1, turn, sc in first 2 sts, [ch 2 (for buttonhole),
sk next sc, sc in next 4 sc] 3 times, sc in each remaining st across.

Row 3: Ch 1, turn, sc in each sc and ch-2 sp to end. Fasten off.

Sew buttons to left front band opposite buttonholes.

Skirt

Rnd 1: Ch 3 (counts as dc), turn, dc in next 2 sts, 2 dc in next st, *dc in next st, 2 dc in next st; repeat from * around; join with sl st in top of beg ch—110 (116, 125) dc.

Rnd 2: Ch 1, turn, (sc, ch 3, 3 dc) in same st as joining, sk next 5 (3, 4) sts, *(sc, ch 3, 3 dc) in next st, sk next 3 sts; repeat from * around; join with sl st in beg sc—27 (29, 31) pattern repeats.

Rnds 3–32: Turn, sl st in next 3 dc (sl st, ch 1, sc, ch 3, 3 dc) in next ch-3 sp, (sc, ch 3, 3 dc) in each remaining ch-3 sp around; join with sl st in beg sc.

Fasten off.

Weave a 50 in. (127 cm) length of ribbon through the stitches of Rnd 1, leaving excess at each end to tie in a bow.

Sleeves (work 2)

Rnd 1: With RS facing, join yarn with sc in back bar of first ch at one underarm, sc in next 1 (2, 1) ch, sc in each st around sleeve opening; join with sl st in beg sc—30 (32, 34) sts.

Rnds 2–7 (8, 9): Ch 1, turn, sc in each st around; join with sl st in beg sc.

Rnd 8 (9, 10): Ch 2 (counts as hdc), hdc in same st as joining, sk next st, *2 hdc in next st, sk next st; repeat from * around; join with sl st in top of beg ch.

Edging Rnd: Sl st in sp between beg ch-2 and next hdc, ch 1, (sc, ch 3, 3 dc) in same sp, (sc, ch 3, 3 dc) in sp between the 2 sts of each 2-hdc group around; join with sl st in beg sc. Fasten off.

Finishing

Weave in ends. Immerse piece in cool water, then squeeze out excess water, taking care not to wring or twist. Place the piece on a flat, covered surface and gently stretch to open lace pattern. Leave until completely dry.

BONNET

Body

Ch 22.

Row 1: (Sc, ch 3, 3 dc) in 2nd ch from hook, sk next 3 ch, [(sc, ch 3, 3 dc) in next ch, sk next 3 ch] 4 times, sc in last ch—5 pattern repeats.

Row 2: Ch 1, turn, sc in first st, ch 3, (sc, ch 3, 3 dc) in each of next 4 ch-3 sps, sc in last ch-3 sp.

Row 3: Ch 1, turn, (sc, ch 3, 3 dc) in first st, (sc, ch 3, 3 dc) in each of next 4 ch-3 sps, sc in last ch-3 sp.

Rows 4–9: Repeat Rows 2–3 three times. Place a marker in the end of the last row (Row 9).

Rows 10–23: Repeat Rows 2–3 seven times.

Row 24: Repeat Row 2.

Row 25: Ch 6 (counts as dc, ch 3), turn, sc in next ch-3 sp, [ch 3, sc in next ch-3 sp] 4 times. Fasten off.

Back

Row 1: With RS facing and working in ends of rows across side edge of body, join yarn with sc around post of marked st at end of Row 9, ch 3, 3 dc around same st, [sk end of next row, (sc, ch 3, 3 dc) around post of st at end of next row] 4 times, sc around post of st at end of next row—5 pattern repeats.

Rows 2–7: Repeat Rows 2 and 3 of body 3 times.

Fasten off.

Matching up row ends of back with row ends of body across one side, sew together. Repeat for opposite side.

Weave a 27 in. (68.5 cm) length of ribbon through spaces around front edge, leaving excess at each end to tie in a bow.

Finishing

Weave in ends. Immerse piece in cool water, then squeeze out excess water, taking care not to wring or twist. Place the piece on a flat, covered surface and gently stretch to open lace pattern. Leave until completely dry.

Heirloom Blessings Christening Gown

SKILL LEVEL

EXPERIENCED

The lacy motifs and feminine drape of this christening gown offer timeless appeal, making this the perfect choice when you want a truly special gown that can be worn by all the girls in the family. The sweet little bonnet made using the same motif found in the skirt of the dress is the crowning accent piece.

YARN

Elann Collection Peruvian Baby Cashmere (60% Baby Alpaca, 30% Merino Wool, 10% Cashmere; 0.88 oz/25 g; 109 yd./100 m)
#0100 Parchment: 7 (8, 9) balls

CROCHET HOOK

U.S. size F-5 (3.75 mm) or size needed to obtain gauge

ADDITIONAL MATERIALS

3 buttons (shown: Blumenthal Lansing La Petite ⅝ in. [16 mm] #843 Rose buttons)
3 yd. (2.75 m) ribbon, ⅛ in. (3 mm) wide
Yarn needle

SIZES

3–6 months (6–12 months, 12–18 months)
Note: Instructions are written for smallest size; changes for larger sizes are given in parentheses.

FINISHED MEASUREMENTS

Chest: 19½ (21, 22½) in.
    [49.5 (53.5, 57) cm]
Length: 24 (24, 24¾) in.
    [61 (61, 63) cm]

GAUGE

15 sc and 18 rows/rounds = 4 in. (10 cm)
Motif rounds 1-4 = 3½ in. (9 cm) in diameter

SPECIAL STITCHES

Beginning cluster (beg-cl): Ch 3, [yarn over, insert hook in indicated sp, yarn over and pull up loop, yarn over and pull through 2 loops on hook] twice, yarn over and pull through all 3 loops on hook.

Ch-3 join: Ch 1, drop loop from hook, insert hook in center ch of corresponding ch-3 sp, pick up dropped loop and pull through, ch 1.

Ch-5 join: Ch 2, drop loop from hook, insert hook in center ch of corresponding ch-5 sp, pick up dropped loop and pull through, ch 2.

Ch-7 join: Ch 3, drop loop from hook, insert hook in center ch of corresponding ch-7 sp, pick up dropped loop and pull through, ch 3.

Ch-9 join: Ch 4, drop loop from hook, insert hook in center ch of corresponding ch-9 sp, pick up dropped loop and pull through, ch 4.

Cluster (cl): [Yarn over, insert hook in indicated sp, yarn over and pull up loop, yarn over and pull through 2 loops on hook] 3 times, yarn over and pull through all 4 loops on hook.

NOTES

Yoke is made first working from top down.

GIRL

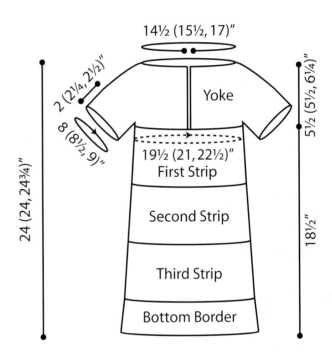

GOWN

Work yoke, sleeve openings, and front edging and buttonhole band as for the boy version.

Collar

Row 1: With RS facing and working in bottom loops of Rnd 1, join yarn with sl st in first st on right front; loosely sl st in each st around neck opening.

Row 2: Ch 2, turn, sl st in 2nd ch from hook, working over sl sts of previous row, sl st in next st, *ch 2, sl st in 2nd ch from hook, sl st in next st; repeat from * to end. Fasten off.

Sleeves (work 2)

Work sleeves as for boy version through Rnd 10—30 (32, 34) sts.

Edging Rnd: Sl st in sp between beg ch-2 and next hdc, ch 5 (counts as dc, ch 2), dc in same sp, (dc, ch 2, dc) in sp between the 2 sts of each 2-hdc group around; join with sl st in 3rd ch of beg ch-5. Fasten off.

Skirt

First Strip

MOTIF 1

Ch 3; join with sl st to form ring.

Rnd 1: Beg-cl in ring, ch 3, (cl in ring, ch 3) 7 times; join with sl st in top of beg-cl—8 cl and 8 ch-3 sps.

Rnd 2: Sl st in next ch-3 sp, ch 1, 3 sc in same sp, ch 1, *3 sc in next ch-3 sp, ch 1; repeat from * around; join with sl st in first sc—24 sc and 8 ch-1 sps.

Rnd 3: Sl st in next st, ch 1, sc in same st, ch 3, sc in next ch-1 sp, ch 3, *sc in center st of next 3-sc group, ch 3, sc in next ch-1 sp, ch 3; repeat from * around; join with sl st in beg sc—16 sc and 16 ch-3 sps.

Rnd 4: (Sl st, ch 1, sc) in next ch-3 sp, sc in next 2 ch-3 sps, (cl, [ch 3, cl] 3 times) in next ch-3 sp, *sc in next 3 ch-3 sps, (cl, [ch 3, cl] 3 times) in next ch-3 sp; repeat from * around; join with sl st in beg sc—16 cl.

Rnd 5: Sl st in next sc (center sc of 3-sc group), ch 8 (counts as dc, ch 5), dc in same st, (sc, ch 3, sc) in next ch-3 sp, (sc, ch 3, sc, ch 5, sc, ch 3, sc) in next ch-3 sp, (sc, ch 3, sc) in next ch-3 sp, sk next sc, *(dc, ch 5, dc) in next sc, (sc, ch 3, sc) in next ch-3 sp, (sc, ch 3, sc, ch 5, sc, ch 3, sc) in next ch-3 sp, (sc, ch 3, sc) in next ch-3 sp, sk next sc; repeat from * around; join with sl st in 3rd ch of beg ch-8. Fasten off.

MOTIFS 2–6

Work same as motif 1 through Rnd 4. Join each motif to previous motif to form a strip as you work Rnd 5.

Rnd 5: Sl st in next sc, ch 8 (counts as dc, ch 5), dc in same st, (sc, ch 3, sc) in next ch-3 sp, (sc, ch 3, sc, ch-5 join, sc, ch-3 join, sc) in next ch-3 sp, (sc, ch-3 join, sc) in next ch-3 sp, sk next sc, (dc, ch-5 join, dc) in next sc, (sc, ch-3 join, sc) in next ch-3 sp, (sc, ch-3 join, sc, ch-5 join, sc, ch 3, sc) in next ch-3 sp, (sc, ch 3, sc) in next ch-3 sp, sk next sc, *(dc, ch 5, dc) in next sc, (sc, ch 3, sc) in next ch-3 sp, (sc, ch 3, sc, ch 5, sc, ch 3, sc) in next ch-3 sp, (sc, ch 3, sc) in next ch-3 sp, sk next sc; repeat from * twice; join with sl st in 3rd ch of beg ch-8. Fasten off.

MOTIF 7

Work same as motif 1 through Rnd 4. Join motif to motif 6 and motif 1 (to turn the strip into a ring) as you work Rnd 5.

Rnd 5: Sl st in next sc, ch 8 (counts as dc, ch 5), dc in same st, (sc, ch 3, sc) in next ch-3 sp, (sc, ch 3, sc, ch-5 join, sc, ch-3 join, sc) in next ch-3 sp, (sc, ch-3 join, sc) in next ch-3 sp, sk next sc, (dc, ch-5 join, dc) in next sc, (sc, ch-3 join, sc) in next ch-3 sp, (sc, ch-3 join, sc, ch-5 join, sc, ch 3, sc) in next ch-3 sp, (sc, ch 3, sc) in next ch-3 sp, sk next sc, (dc, ch 5, dc) in next sc, (sc, ch 3, sc) in next ch-3 sp, (sc, ch 3, sc, ch-5 join, sc, ch-3 join, sc) in next ch-3 sp, (sc, ch-3 join, sc) in next ch-3 sp, sk next sc, (dc, ch-5 join, dc) in next sc, (sc, ch-3 join, sc) in next ch-3 sp, (sc, ch-3 join, sc, ch-5 join, sc, ch 3, sc) in next ch-3 sp, (sc, ch 3, sc) in next ch-3 sp, sk next sc, join with sl st in 3rd ch of beg ch-8. Fasten off.

Second Strip

MOTIF 1

Work same as motif 1 of first strip through Rnd 4. Join to the first motif of first strip as you work Rnd 5, as follows:

Rnd 5: Sl st in next sc, ch 10 (counts as dc, ch 7), dc in same st, (sc, ch 5, sc) in next ch-3 sp, (sc, ch 5, sc, ch-7 join, sc, ch-5 join, sc) in next ch-3 sp, (sc, ch-5 join, sc) in next ch-3 sp, sk next sc, (dc, ch-7 join, dc) in next sc, (sc, ch-5 join, sc) in next ch-3 sp, (sc, ch-5 join, sc, ch-7 join, sc, ch 5, sc) in next ch-3 sp, (sc, ch 5, sc) in next ch-3 sp, sk next sc, *(dc, ch 7, dc) in next sc, (sc, ch 5, sc) in next ch-3 sp, (sc, ch 5, sc, ch 7, sc, ch 5, sc) in next ch-3 sp, (sc, ch 5, sc) in next ch-3 sp, sk next sc; repeat from * twice; join with sl st in 3rd ch of beg ch-10. Fasten off.

MOTIFS 2–6

Work same as motif 1 of first strip through Rnd 4. Join each motif to prev motif of this strip and also to corresponding motif of first strip as you work Rnd 5, as follows:

Rnd 5: Sl st in next sc, ch 10 (counts as dc, ch 7), dc in same st, (sc, ch 5, sc) in next ch-3 sp, (sc, ch 5, sc, ch-7 join, sc, ch-5 join, sc) in next ch-3 sp, (sc, ch-5 join, sc) in next ch-3 sp, sk next sc, (dc, ch-7 join, dc) in next sc, (sc, ch-5 join, sc) in next ch-3 sp, (sc, ch-5 join, sc, ch-7 join, sc, ch-5 join, sc) in next ch-3 sp, (sc, ch-5 join, sc) in next ch-3 sp, sk next sc, (dc, ch-7 join, dc) in next sc, (sc, ch-5 join, sc) in next ch-3 sp, (sc, ch-5 join, sc, ch-7 join, sc, ch 5, sc) in next ch-3 sp, (sc, ch 5, sc) in next ch-3 sp, sk next sc, (dc, ch 7, dc) in next sc, (sc, ch 5, sc) in next ch-3 sp, (sc, ch 5, sc, ch 7, sc, ch 5, sc) in next ch-3 sp, (sc, ch 5, sc) in next ch-3 sp, sk next sc; join with sl st in 3rd ch of beg ch-10. Fasten off.

MOTIF 7

Work same as motif 1 of first strip through Rnd 4. Join to prev motif of this strip, to first motif of this strip, and to corresponding motif of first strip as you work Rnd 5, as follows:

Rnd 5: Sl st in next sc, ch 10 (counts as dc, ch 7), dc in same st, (sc, ch 5, sc) in next ch-3 sp, (sc, ch 5, sc, ch-7 join, sc, ch-5 join, sc) in next ch-3 sp, (sc, ch-5 join, sc) in next ch-3 sp, sk next sc, (dc, ch-7 join, dc) in next sc, (sc, ch-5 join, sc) in next ch-3 sp, *(sc, ch-5 join, sc, ch-7 join, sc, ch-5 join, sc) in next ch-3 sp, (sc, ch-5 join, sc) in next ch-3 sp, sk next sc, (dc, ch-7 join, dc) in next sc, (sc, ch-5 join, sc) in next ch-3 sp; repeat from * once more, (sc, ch-5 join, sc, ch-7 join, sc, ch 5, sc) in next ch-3 sp, (sc, ch 5, sc) in next ch-3 sp, sk next sc; join with sl st in 3rd ch of beg ch-10. Fasten off.

Third Strip
MOTIF 1

Work same as motif 1 of first strip through Rnd 4. Join to the first motif of second strip as you work Rnd 5, as follows:

Rnd 5: Sl st in next sc, ch 12 (counts as dc, ch 9), dc in same st, (sc, ch 7, sc) in next ch-3 sp, (sc, ch 7, sc, ch-9 join, sc, ch-7 join, sc) in next ch-3 sp, (sc, ch-7 join, sc) in next ch-3 sp, sk next sc, (dc, ch-9 join, dc) in next sc, (sc, ch-7 join, sc) in next ch-3 sp, (sc, ch-7 join, sc, ch-9 join, sc, ch 7, sc) in next ch-3 sp, (sc, ch 7, sc) in next ch-3 sp, sk next sc, *(dc, ch 9, dc) in next sc, (sc, ch 7, sc) in next ch-3 sp, (sc, ch 7, sc, ch 9 sc, ch 7, sc) in next ch-3 sp, (sc, ch 7, sc) in next ch-3 sp, sk next sc; repeat from * twice; join with sl st in 3rd ch of beg ch-12. Fasten off.

MOTIFS 2–6

Work same as motif 1 of first strip through Rnd 4. Join each motif to prev motif of this strip and also to corresponding motif of first strip as you work Rnd 5, as follows:

Rnd 5: Sl st in next sc, ch 12 (counts as dc, ch 9), dc in same st, (sc, ch 7, sc) in next ch-3 sp, (sc, ch 7, sc, ch-9 join, sc, ch-7 join, sc) in next ch-3 sp, (sc, ch-7 join, sc) in next ch-3 sp, sk next sc, (dc, ch-9 join, dc) in next sc, (sc, ch-7 join, sc) in next ch-3 sp, (sc, ch-7 join, sc, ch-9 join, sc, ch-7 join, sc) in next ch-3 sp, (sc, ch-7 join, sc) in next ch-3 sp, sk next sc, (dc, ch-9 join, dc) in next sc, (sc, ch-7 join, sc) in next ch-3 sp, (sc, ch-7 join, sc, ch-9 join, sc, ch 7, sc) in next ch-3 sp, (sc, ch 7, sc) in next ch-3 sp, sk next sc, (dc, ch 9, dc) in next sc, (sc, ch 7, sc) in next ch-3 sp, (sc, ch 7, sc, ch 9, sc, ch 7, sc) in next ch-3 sp, (sc, ch 7, sc) in next ch-3 sp, sk next sc; join with sl st in 3rd ch of beg ch-12. Fasten off.

MOTIF 7

Work same as motif 1 of first strip through Rnd 4. Join to prev motif of this strip, to first motif of this strip, and to corresponding motif of first strip as you work Rnd 5, as follows:

Rnd 5: Sl st in next sc, ch 12 (counts as dc, ch 9), dc in same st, (sc, ch 7, sc) in next ch-3 sp, (sc, ch 7, sc, ch-9 join, sc, ch-7 join, sc) in next ch-3 sp, (sc, ch-7 join, sc) in next ch-3 sp, sk next sc, (dc, ch-9 join, dc) in next sc, (sc, ch-7 join, sc) in next ch-3 sp, *(sc, ch-7 join, sc, ch-9 join, sc, ch-7 join, sc) in next ch-3 sp, (sc, ch-7 join, sc) in next ch-3 sp, sk next sc, (dc, ch-9 join, dc) in next sc, (sc, ch-7 join, sc) in next ch-3 sp; repeat from * once more, (sc, ch-7 join, sc, ch-9 join, sc, ch 7, sc) in next ch-3 sp, (sc, ch 7, sc) in next ch-3 sp, sk next sc; join with sl st in 3rd ch of beg ch-12. Fasten off.

Top Edge of Skirt

Working in ch-sps around top of first strip, join yarn with sl st in center of any join between motifs; ch 4 (counts as dc, ch 1), dc in same sp, dc in next ch-3 sp, ch 3, dc in next ch-3 sp, (dc, ch 3, dc) in next ch-5 sp, dc in next ch-3 sp, ch 3, dc in next ch-3 sp, *(dc, ch 3, dc) in center of next join, dc in next ch-3 sp, ch 3, dc in next ch-3 sp, (dc, ch 3, dc) in next ch-5 sp, dc in next ch-3 sp, ch 3, dc in next ch-3 sp; repeat from * around; join with sl st in 3rd ch of beg ch-4. Fasten off.

Attach Yoke to Skirt: With RS facing, join yarn with sc in any st on last rnd of yoke, (ch-3 join working join in next ch-sp of top of skirt, sc) in same st, sk next 2 sts, *(sc, ch-3 join, sc) in next st, sk next 2 sts; repeat from * around, skipping only 1 st at end of rnd for smallest size; join with sl st in beg sc. Fasten off.

Weave a 50 in. (127 cm) length of ribbon through stitches of rnd just worked, leaving excess at each end to tie in a bow.

Bottom Border

Rnd 1: Working in sps at bottom of skirt, join yarn with sl st in center of any join between motifs, ch 6, (counts as dc, ch 3), (dc, [ch 3, dc] twice) in same sp, (dc, ch 3, dc) in each ch-sp up to next join, *(dc, [ch 3, dc] 3 times) in center of join, (dc, ch 3, dc) in each ch-sp up to next join; repeat from * around; join with sl st in 3rd ch of beg ch-6.

Rnds 2–4: Sl st in next ch-3 sp, ch 6, dc in same sp, (dc, ch 3, dc) in each ch-3 sp around; join with sl st in 3rd ch of beg ch-6.

Fasten off.

Finishing

Weave in all ends. Immerse the piece in cool water, squeeze out excess water, taking care not to wring or twist. Place on a flat, covered surface and gently stretch to open up lace pattern. Leave until completely dry.

BONNET
Front Strip

Make three motifs as for motif 1 of skirt, joining them into a strip as you work Rnd 5 of the second and third motifs.

Back

Make same as motif 1 of skirt through Rnd 4—16 cl.

Rnd 5 (assembly round): Sl st in next sc, ch 8 (counts as dc, ch 5), dc in same st, (sc, ch 3, sc) in next ch-3 sp; joining to first motif of front strip, (sc, ch 3, sc, ch-5 join, sc, ch-3 join, sc) in next ch-3 sp, (sc, ch-3 join, sc) in next ch-3 sp, sk next sc, (dc, ch-5 join, dc) in next sc, (sc, ch-3 join, sc) in next ch-3 sp; joining to second motif of front strip beginning in ch-5 join at center of corner, (sc, ch-3 join, sc, ch-5 join, sc, ch-3 join, sc) in next ch-3 sp, (sc, ch-3 join, sc) in next ch-3 sp, sk next sc, (dc, ch-5 join, dc) in next sc, (sc, ch-3 join, sc) in next ch-3 sp; joining to third motif of front strip beginning in ch-5 join at center of corner, (sc, ch-3 join, sc, ch-5 join, sc, ch-3 join, sc) in next ch-3 sp, (sc, ch-3 join, sc) in next ch-3 sp, sk next sc, (dc, ch-5 join, dc) in next sc, (sc, ch-3 join, sc) in next ch-3 sp, (sc, ch-3 join, sc, ch-5 join, sc, ch 3, sc) in next ch-3 sp, (sc, ch 3, sc) in next ch-3 sp, sk next sc; join with sl st in 3rd ch of beg ch-8. Fasten off.

Front Border

Row 1: Join yarn with sl st in ch-5 sp at beginning of unjoined long edge of front strip, ch 3 (counts as dc), [(dc, ch 3, dc) in next 5 ch-sps, dc in center of join between motifs] twice, (dc, ch 3, dc) in next 5 ch-sps, dc in next sp.

Rnd 1: Ch 1, turn, sc in first st, (sc, ch 3, sc) in each ch-3 sp across front, sc in last st, (sc, ch 3, sc) in each ch-sp across sides and back; join with sl st in first sc.

Rnd 2: Ch 1, sc in first st, (sc, [ch 3, sc] 3 times) in next 15 ch-3 sps, sk next sc, sc in next sc, 3 sc in each ch-3 sp to end; join with sl st in first sc. Fasten off.

Weave a 27 in. (68.5 cm) length of ribbon through the spaces around the front edge, leaving excess at each end to tie in a bow.

Finishing

Weave in all ends. Immerse the piece in cool water, squeeze out excess water, taking care not to wring or twist. Place on a flat, covered surface and gently stretch to open up lace pattern. Leave until completely dry.

CHAPTER TWO

February

Love Is in the Air

These February outfits naturally feature a heart in honor of Valentine's Day. If you don't celebrate Valentine's Day, you can let the heart symbolize the love you have for your precious baby or simply omit it.

My Heart Is Yours Boy Cardigan Set

SKILL LEVEL

EASY

The love shared between you and your little boy will be clear to all with this precious little sweater. Every little boy needs an outfit in the classic blue and red color combination.

YARN
Berroco Weekend DK (75% Acrylic, 25% Peruvian Cotton;
    3.5 oz/100 g; 268 yd./247 m)
#2944 Starry Night (A): 2 hanks
#2955 Reddy (B): 1 hank

CROCHET HOOK
U.S. size H-8 (5 mm) or size needed to obtain gauge

ADDITIONAL MATERIALS
Stitch markers
Yarn needle
4 flat navy blue buttons, ¾ in. (19 mm) in diameter
Sewing needle and matching thread

SIZES
3 months (6 months, 9 months, 12 months)
Note: Instructions are given for smallest size; changes for
    larger sizes are given in parentheses.

FINISHED MEASUREMENTS
Cardigan Chest: 17 (18, 19, 20) in. [43 (45.5, 48.5, 51) cm]
Cardigan Length: 7½ (8, 8½, 9) in. [19 (20.5, 21.5, 23) cm],
    including bottom band
Bootie Length: 4¼ in. (11.5 cm)

GAUGE
14½ sc and 17 rows/rnds = 4 in. (10 cm)

NOTES
Sweater is made from the bottom up, working the body
in one piece and then splitting for the left front, the back,
and the right front. Sleeves are worked directly into armhole openings.

CARDIGAN
Body
With A, ch 63 (66, 70, 73).
Row 1 (RS): Sc in 2nd ch from hook and in each ch
    across—62 (65, 69, 72) sc.
Rows 2–17: Ch 1, turn, sc in each st across.

Left Front
Row 1 (WS): Ch 1, turn, sc in first 15 (16, 17, 18) sts;
    leave remaining sts unworked for back and right
    front.
Rows 2–4: Ch 1, turn, sc in each st across.
Row 5: Ch 1, turn, sc2tog, sc in each st across—14 (15,
    16, 17) sts.
Row 6: Ch 1, turn, sc in each st across.
Rows 7–8 (10, 12, 14): Repeat last 2 rows 1 (2, 3, 4)
    more times—13 sts.
Row 9 (11, 13, 15): Ch 1, turn, sc2tog, sc in each st
    across—12 sts.
Row 10 (12, 14, 16): Ch 1, turn, sc in each st across
    to last 2 sts, sc2tog—11 sts.
Next 4 Rows: Repeat last 2 rows 2 more times—7 sts.
Fasten off.

Back
Row 1 (WS): With WS facing, join A with sc in first
    unworked st of last row of body after left front; sc
    in next 31 (32, 34, 35) sts; leave remaining sts
    unworked for right front—32 (33, 35, 36) sts.
Rows 2–14 (16, 18, 20): Ch 1, turn, sc in each st across.
Fasten off.

Right Front
Row 1 (WS): With WS facing, join A with sc in first
    unworked st of last row of body after back; sc in
    each remaining st across—15 (16, 17, 18) sts.
Rows 2–4: Ch 1, turn, sc in each st across.
Row 5: Ch 1, turn, sc in each st across to last 2 sts,
    sc2tog—14 (15, 16, 17) sts.
Row 6: Ch 1, turn, sc in each st across.
Rows 7–8 (10, 12, 14): Repeat last 2 rows 1 (2, 3, 4)
    more times—13 sts.
Row 9 (11, 13, 15): Ch 1, turn, sc in each st across to
    last 2 sts, sc2tog—12 sts.
Row 10 (12, 14, 16): Ch 1, turn, sc2tog, sc in each st
    across—11 sts.
Next 4 Rows: Repeat last 2 rows 2 more times—7 sts.
Fasten off.
Sew shoulder seams.

Bottom Band

Row 1 (RS): With RS facing and working in bottom loops of Row 1 of body, join B with sl st in first st, ch 3 (counts as first dc), dc in each st across—62 (65, 69, 72) sts. Do not fasten off.

Front Edging

Row 1 (RS): Do not turn, ch 1; working in ends of rows up right front edge, 2 sc in end of first row (row 1 of bottom band), sc in ends of next 16 rows, 3 sc in end of next row, place a marker in center sc of 3 sc just made, sc in ends of next 14 (16, 18, 20) rows, sc in each st across back neck; working in ends of rows down left front edge, sc in ends of next 14 (16, 18, 20) rows, 3 sc in end of next row, place a marker in center sc of 3 sc just made, sc in ends of next 16 rows, 2 sc in end of last row—88 (93, 99, 104) sts.

Row 2: Ch 1, turn, [sc in each st to marked st, 3 sc in marked st] twice, sc in each st across—92 (97, 103, 108) sts.

Do not fasten off.

Button Band

Row 1 (RS): Ch 1, turn, sc in each st to marked st, sc in marked st—21 sts.

Rows 2–3: Ch 1, turn, sc in each st across.

Fasten off.

Buttonhole Band

Row 1 (RS): With RS facing, join B with sc in marked st on left front edge, *ch 1, sk next st, sc in next 4 sts; repeat from * across—4 ch-1 sps.

Row 2: Ch 1, turn, sc in each sc and ch-1 sp across—21 sts.

Row 3: Ch 1, turn, sc in each st across. Fasten off.

Sleeves (work 2)

Rnd 1 (RS): With RS facing, working in ends of rows around armhole opening, join A with sc in end of first row at underarm, sc in end of each row around; join with sl st in beg sc—28 (32, 36, 40) sc.

Rnd 2: Ch 1, turn, [sc2tog] 3 times, sc in each st around to last 3 sts, [sc2tog] 3 times; join with sl st in beg sc—22 (26, 30, 34) sts.

Rnd 3: Ch 1, turn, sc in each sc around; join with sl st in beg sc.

Repeat last 2 rnds 0 (0, 1, 1) more time(s)—22 (26, 24, 28) sts.

Next 20 (22, 22, 24) Rnds: Ch 1, turn, sc in each sc around; join with sl st in beg sc.

Fasten off.

Cuff

Rnd 1 (RS): With RS facing, join B with sc in any st; sc in each st around, evenly spacing 2 (6, 4, 8) sc2togs around round; join with sl st in beg sc—20 sts.

Next 2 (2, 4, 4) Rnds: Ch 1, sc in each st around; join with sl st in beg sc.

Fasten off.

Heart

With B, ch 2.

Row 1: Work 3 sc in 2nd ch from hook—3 sc.

Row 2: Ch 1, turn, 2 sc in first st, sc in next st, 2 sc in last st—5 sc.

Row 3: Ch 1, turn, 2 sc in first st, sc in next 3 sts, 2 sc in last st—7 sc.

Rows 4–5: Ch 1, turn, sc in each st across.

Row 6: Ch 1, turn, sc in first st, 3 dc in each of next 2 sts, sl st in next st, 3 dc in each of next 2 sts, sc in last st.

Border: Do not turn; sc in end of next 5 rows, (sc, ch 2, sc in 2nd ch from hook (picot made), sc) in bottom loop of row 1, sc in end of next 5 rows, sl st in first st of row 6. Fasten off, leaving a long tail for sewing.

Finishing

Weave in ends. Appliqué the heart to the left front of the sweater, sewing around the edge of the heart as shown in photo. Sew buttons to button band opposite buttonholes.

Rnd 2: Ch 1, 2 sc in first st, *sc in next 10 sts, 2 sc in next 3 sts; repeat from * once more; join with sl st in beg sc—34 sc.

Rnd 3: Ch 1, 2 sc in first st, 2 sc in next st, sc in next 9 sts, hdc in next 2 sts, 2 hdc in next 5 sts, hdc in next 2 sts, sc in next 9 sts, 2 sc in next 2 sts, sc in next 3 sts; join with sl st in beg sc—43 sts.

Rnd 4: Ch 1, 2 sc in first st, sc in next 12 sts, hdc in next 3 sts, 2 hdc in next st, [hdc in next st, 2 hdc in next st] 4 times, hdc in next 2 sts, sc in next 12 sts, 2 sc in next st, sc in last 3 sts; join with sl st in beg sc—50 sts.

Rnd 5: Ch 1, working in BLO, sc in each st around; join with sl st in beg sc.

Sides

Rnd 6: Ch 1, sc in each st around; join with sl st in beg sc.

Rnd 7: Ch 1, sc2tog, sc in next 4 sts, sc2tog 3 times, sc in next 22 sts, sc2tog 3 times, sc in next 4 sts, sc2tog, sc in next 4 sts; join with sl st in beg sc—42 sc.

Ankle

Rnd 1: Ch 1, sc2tog twice, sc in next 4 sts, ch 6, sk next 22 sts, mark last skipped st, sc in next 4 sts, sc2tog twice, sc in next 4 sts; join with sl st in beg sc—16 sc.

Rnd 2: Ch 1, sc in each st and ch around; join with sl st in beg sc—22 sc.

Rnd 3: Ch 1, sc in first 6 sts, working in BLO, sc in next 6 sts, sc in next 10 sts; join with sl st in beg sc.

Rnds 4–7: Repeat Rnd 2 four times.

Fasten off.

BOOTIES

Sole

With A, ch 13.

Rnd 1: Sc in 2nd ch from hook and in next 10 ch, 3 sc in last ch; working in bottom loops of starting ch, sc in next 10 sts, 3 sc in last st; join with sl st in beg sc—27 sc.

Edging

Rnd 1 (RS): With RS facing, join B with sc in any st, sc in each st around; join with sl st in beg sc.

Rnd 2: Ch 1, sc in each st around; join with sl st in beg sc. Fasten off.

Upper

Row 1 (RS): With RS facing, join A with sl st in marked st; working in bottom loops of ch, sc in next 6 ch, sl st in next 2 skipped sts on last rnd of sole.

Rows 2–9: Turn, sk the sl sts, sc in next 6 sts, sl st in next 2 skipped sts on last rnd of sole.

Fasten off, leaving a long tail for sewing.

Finishing

Sew the opening between the last row of the upper and the toe edging closed. Weave in ends.

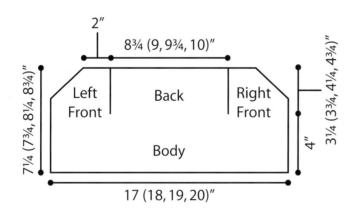

Notes: Body is shown before bottom band is worked. Sleeves are worked directly into armholes, after shoulders are seamed.

Queen of Hearts Girl Cardigan Set

SKILL LEVEL

EASY

Your little girl is sure to be the queen of her daddy's heart. What better way to express that than with a cute little headband full of hearts and a matching sweater and bootie set?

19

YARN
Berroco Weekend DK (75% Acrylic,
   25% Peruvian Cotton; 3.5 oz/100 g;
   268 yd./247 m)
#2911 Tea Rose (A): 2 hanks
#2955 Reddy (B): 1 hank

CROCHET HOOK
U.S. size H-8 (5 mm) or size needed
   to obtain gauge

ADDITIONAL MATERIALS
Stitch markers
Yarn needle
4 flat pink buttons, ¾ in. (19 mm)
   in diameter
Sewing needle and matching thread

SIZES
3 months (6 months, 9 months,
   12 months)
Note: Instructions are given for smallest
   size; changes for larger sizes are
   given in parentheses.

FINISHED MEASUREMENTS
Cardigan Chest: 17 (18, 19, 20) in.
   [43 (45.5, 48.5, 51) cm]
Cardigan Length: 7½ (8, 8½, 9) in.
   [19 (20.5, 21.5, 23) cm], including
   bottom band
Bootie Length: 4¼ in. (11.5 cm)

GAUGE
14½ sc and 17 rows/rnds = 4 in.
   (10 cm)

SPECIAL STITCH
Front post treble crochet (FPtr): Yarn
over twice, insert hook around post
of next stitch from front to back and
then to front again, yarn over and
draw up a loop, [yarn over and draw
through 2 loops on hook] 3 times.

NOTES
Sweater is made from the bottom up, working the body
in one piece, then splitting for the left front, then the
back, then the right front. Sleeves are worked directly
into armhole openings.

CARDIGAN

Work same as boy version to end of front edging—92 (97, 103, 108) sts in front edging. Do not fasten off.

Buttonhole Band

Row 1 (RS): Ch 1, turn, [sc in next 4 sts, ch 1, sk next st] 4 times, sc in next st; leave remaining sts unworked— 4 ch-1 sps.

Row 2: Ch 1, turn, sc in each sc and ch-1 sp across— 21 sts.

Row 3: Ch 1, turn, sc in each st across.
Fasten off.

Button Band

Row 1 (RS): With RS facing, join B with sc in marked st on left front edge, sc in each remaining st across— 21 sts.

Rows 2–3: Ch 1, turn, sc in each st across.
Fasten off.
Work sleeves, cuffs, and heart as for boy version.

Finishing

Weave in ends. Appliqué the heart to the left front of the sweater, sewing around the edge of the heart as shown in photo. Sew buttons to button band opposite buttonholes.

BOOTIES

Work same as boy version until end of ankle. Fasten off.

Edging

Working in FLO, join B with sc in any st, 2 sc in same st as joining, 3 sc in each st around; join with sl st in beg sc. Fasten off.
Work upper as for boy version.

Finishing

Sew opening between last row of upper and toe edging closed. Weave in ends.

HEADBAND

With A, ch 57.

Rnd 1: Sc in 2nd ch from hook and in each ch across; join with sl st in beg sc—56 sc.

Rnd 2: Ch 1, turn, sc in each st around; join with sl st in beg sc.

Rnd 3: Ch 3, working in BLO, dc in each st around; join with sl st in top of beg ch.

Rnd 4: Repeat Rnd 2. Do not fasten off.

Assembly: Cut a 16 in. (40.5 cm) length of elastic. Form a ring with the elastic, overlapping the ends ½ in. (13 mm), sew ends together. Slide headband over elastic. Working through sts of last rnd and bottom lps of rnd 1 at same time, ch 1, sl st in each st across. Fasten off.

Heart Edging

Rnd 1: Join B with sl st in any st of assembly round, mark this st, *sk next st, FPtr around sc of previous rnd directly below next st, 5 dc in marked st, remove marker, sk next st, sl st in next st, sk next st, 5 dc in next st, FPtr around same st as previous FPtr, sl st in same st as 5 dc, sl st in next 3 sts, mark last st; repeat from * around omitting last sl st, fasten off.

Finishing

Weave in ends.

March
Luck of the Irish

Many of us, whether or not we have an Irish heritage, carry on the tradition of wearing green on March 17, St. Patrick's Day. With this sweater and hat set for March, your baby can celebrate St. Patrick's Day right along with you. The adorable sweaters would also work well in another color combination (perhaps the colors of your favorite sports team).

Galway Boy and Derry Girl Sweater and Hat Set

With this set, your baby can watch his or her first St. Patrick's Day parade in warm comfort. The Galway sweater features a dark green sweater body with light green trim at the neck, sleeves, and hem, while the Derry sweater switches the main and contrasting colors. The hat picks up the accent color in the sweater.

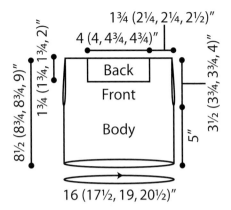

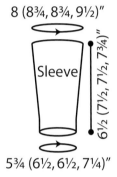

Notes: Body is shown before bottom band is worked. Sleeves are worked directly into armholes after shoulders are seamed.

YARN
Caron Simply Soft (100% Acrylic; 6 oz/170 g; 315 yd./288 m)
Boy version
#9707 Dark Sage (MC): 1 skein
#9705 Sage (CC): 1 skein
Girl version
#9705 Sage (MC): 1 skein
#9707 Dark Sage (CC): 1 skein

CROCHET HOOK
U.S. size I-9 (5.5 mm) or size needed to obtain gauge

ADDITIONAL MATERIALS
Yarn needle

SIZES
0–3 months (3–6 months, 6–9 months, 9–12 months)
Note: Instructions are given for smallest size; changes for larger sizes are given in parentheses.

FINISHED MEASUREMENTS
Sweater
Chest: 16 (17½, 19, 20½) in. [40.5 (44.5, 48.5, 52) cm]
Length: 9½ (9¾, 9¾, 10) in. [24 (25, 25, 25.5) cm], including bottom band
Hat
Circumference: 17 in. (43 cm)
Height: 4 in. (10 cm)

GAUGE
11 sts and 12 rnds/rows = 4 in. (10 cm)

SPECIAL STITCH
Front post double crochet (FPdc): Yarn over, insert hook around post of next stitch from front to back and then to front again, yarn over and draw up loop, [yarn over and draw through 2 loops on hook] twice.

NOTES
Sweater is worked in joined rnds beginning at lower edge. Piece is divided at underarm and front and back worked separately.

SWEATER
Body
With MC, ch 44 (48, 52, 56), join with sl st to form ring.
Rnd 1 (RS): Ch 1, sc in each ch around, join with sl st in beg sc—44 (48, 52, 56) sc.
Rnd 2: Ch 1, turn, sc in first st, dc in next st, *sc in next st, dc in next st; repeat from * around, join with sl st in beg sc—22 (24, 26, 28) sc and 22 (24, 26, 28) dc.
Rnd 3: Ch 1, turn, FPdc in first st, sc in next st, *FPdc in next st, sc in next st; repeat from * around, join with sl st in first st.
Rnds 4–15: Repeat last 2 rnds six times.

Front

Row 1 (WS): Ch 1, turn, sc in first st, *dc in next st, sc in next st; repeat from * 10 (11, 12, 13) times leaving remaining sts unworked—11 (12, 13, 14) sc and 10 (11, 12, 13) dc.

Row 2: Ch 1, turn, sc in first st, *FPdc in next st, sc in next st; repeat from * across.

Row 3: Ch 1, turn, sc in first st, *dc in next st, sc in next st; repeat from * across.

Repeat last 2 rows you have worked a total of 5 (6, 6, 6) rows from beginning of front.

Left Shoulder

> **NOTE** To "work in pattern as established," continue to alternate [FPdc, sc] rows and [dc, sc] rows. Make sure that you are working the scs into scs, dcs into FPdcs, and FPdcs into dcs of the previous row.

Row 1: Ch 1, turn, work in pattern as established over the first 5 (6, 6, 7) sts, leaving remaining sts unworked—5 (6, 6, 7) sts.

Next 4 (4, 4, 5) Rows: Ch 1, turn, work in pattern as established across.

Fasten off.

Right Shoulder

Row 1: With WS facing, sk next 11 (11, 13, 13) sts on last row of back (for neck), join MC with sc in next st, work in pattern as established to end of row—5 (6, 6, 7) sts.

Next 4 (4, 4, 5) Rows: Ch 1, turn, work in pattern as established across.

Fasten off.

Back

Row 1: With WS facing, sk next unworked st on last rnd of body (for underarm), join MC with sc in next st, *dc in next st, sc in next st; repeat from *10 (11, 12, 13) times—11 (12, 13, 14) sc and 10 (11, 12, 13) dc.

Row 2: Ch 1, turn, sc in first st, *FPdc in next st, sc in next st; repeat from * across.

Row 3: Ch 1, turn, sc in first st, *dc in next st, sc in next st; repeat from * across.

Repeat last 2 rows until you have worked a total of 10 (11, 11, 12) rows from beginning of back. Fasten off.

Sleeve (work 2)

Rnd 1: With WS facing, join MC with sc in skipped st at either underarm, dc in same st, working in row ends around armhole opening; *sc in next row, dc in next row; repeat from * around, join with sl st in beg sc—11 (12, 12, 13) sc and 11 (12, 12, 13) dc.

Rnd 2: Ch 1, turn, FPdc in first st, sc in next st, *FPdc in next st, sc in next st; repeat from * around, join with sl st in first st.

Rnd 3: Ch 1, turn, sc in first st, dc in next st, *sc in next st, dc in next st; repeat from * around, join with sl st in beg sc.

Repeat last 2 rnds until piece measures about 5½ (6½, 6½, 6¾) in. [14 (16.5, 16.5, 17) cm] from beginning. Fasten off. Repeat on other side of sweater.

Cuff

Rnd 1: With RS facing, join CC with sc in any st; sc in each st around, working 6 sc2tog evenly spaced around round; join with sl st in beg sc—16 (18, 18, 20) sc.

Rnds 2–3: Ch 1, sc in each st around, join with sl st in beg sc.

Fasten off.

Sew shoulder seams.

Neck Band and Collar

Rnd 1: With RS facing, join MC with sc in neck edge at a shoulder seam, sc in each st and row end all the way around neck edge, join with sl st in beg sc. Fasten off.

Rnd 2: With RS facing, join CC with sc in any st of neck edge, sc in each st around, join with sl st in beg sc.

Rnds 3–4: Ch 1, sc in each st around, join with sl st in beg sc.

Fasten off.

Bottom Band

Rnd 1: With RS facing, working in bottom loops of Rnd 1 of body, join CC with sc in any st, sc in each st around, join with sl st in beg sc.

Rnds 2–3: Ch 1, sc in each st around, join with sl st in beg sc.

Fasten off.

Finishing

Weave in ends.

HAT

Holding 2 strands of CC together, ch 4, join with sl st to form ring.

Rnd 1: Ch 3, 15 dc in ring, join with sl st in top of beg ch—16 dc.

Rnd 2: Ch 3, dc in same st as joining, 2 dc in each st around, join with sl st in top of beg ch—32 dc.

Rnd 3: Ch 3, dc in same st as joining, dc in next 3 sts, *2 dc in next st, dc in next 3 sts; repeat from * around, join with sl st in top of beg ch—40 dc.

Rnd 4: Ch 3, working in BLO, dc in each st around, join with sl st in top of beg ch.

Rnd 5: Ch 1, turn, sc in first st, dc in next st, *sc in next st, dc in next st; repeat from * around, join with sl st in beg sc.

Rnd 6: Ch 1, turn, FPdc in first st, sc in next st, *FPdc in next st, sc in next st; repeat from * around, join with sl st in first st.

Rnds 7–12: Repeat last 2 rnds 3 more times.

Brim

Row 1: Ch 1, working in FLO, sk first st, sc in next 5 sts, [2 dc in next st, dc in next st] 7 times, sc in next 5 sts, ch 1, sk next st, sl st in next st, leaving remaining sts unworked—10 sc and 21 dc.

Row 2: Ch 1, turn; sk the sl st, ch-1 sp, and next sc; sc2tog, sc in next 4 sts, dc in next 17 sts, sc in next 4 sts, sc2tog, ch 1, sl st in beg ch—10 sc and 17 dc.

Fasten off.

Finishing

Weave in ends.

CHAPTER FOUR

April

Think Spring!

The soft pastels of these outfits combined with bright accent colors bring to mind various images of spring: April showers, Easter egg hunts, the blooming of the first spring flowers, and even the return of our favorite songbirds.

Bold as a Blue Jay
Boy Romper and Hat

Your baby boy's bright
and bubbly personality
will come shining through
in this one-piece romper
and hat set. This outfit is
the perfect introduction
to using multiple colors in
your work, as you crochet
each piece in a single color,
adding the accent colors in
solid blocks after crochet-
ing the main piece.

YARN

Red Heart Anne Geddes Baby (80% Acrylic,
   20% Nylon; 3.5 oz/100 g; 340 yd./310 m)
#801 Bluebell (A): 2 balls
#827 Bluejay (B): 1 ball

CROCHET HOOK

U.S. size F-5 (3.75 mm) or size needed
   to obtain gauge

ADDITIONAL MATERIALS

Stitch marker
Yarn needle
6 sew-on snaps, size 4/0

SIZES

3 (6, 9, 12) months
Note: Instructions are given for smallest
   size; changes for larger sizes are
   given in parentheses.

FINISHED MEASUREMENTS

Chest: 17¼ (18¼, 19½, 20½) in.
   [44 (46.5, 49.5, 52) cm]
Length: 12¼ (13¾, 15¾, 17¼) in.
   [31 (35, 40, 44) cm]

GAUGE

14 sc and 16 rows sc = 4 in. (10 cm)

BOY

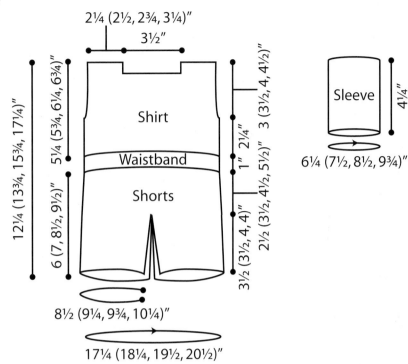

Note: Sleeves are worked directly into
armholes after shoulders are seamed.

SPECIAL STITCH

Front post double crochet (FPdc): Yarn over, insert hook
around post of next stitch from front to back and then
to front again, yarn over and draw up loop, [yarn over
and draw through 2 loops on hook] twice.

NOTES

1. Shirt body is made from the waist up, then split for
   front and back with shoulders seamed and sleeves
   worked directly into armholes.
2. Shorts are worked down from the waist, then split
   for legs.

ROMPER

Shirt

With A, ch 60 (64, 68, 72), join with sl st to form ring,
   taking care not to twist.

Rnd 1: Ch 1, sc in each ch around, join with sl st in beg
   sc—60 (64, 68, 72) sc.

Rnds 2–9: Ch 1, turn, sc in first st and each st around,
   join with sl st in beg sc.

Front

Row 1: Ch 1, turn, sc in first 28 (30, 32, 34) sts, leaving
   remaining sts unworked—28 (30, 32, 34) sc.

Rows 2–9: Ch 1, turn, sc in each st across.

FIRST SHOULDER

Row 1: Ch 1, turn, sc in first 8 (9, 10, 11) sts leaving remaining sts unworked—8 (9, 10, 11) sc.

Rows 2–3 (5, 7, 9): Ch 1, turn, sc in each st across.

Fasten off.

SECOND SHOULDER

Row 1: Sk next 12 sts on last row of front; join A with sc in next st, sc in next 7 (8, 9, 10) sts.

Rows 2–3 (5, 7, 9): Ch 1, turn, sc in each st across.

Fasten off.

Back

Row 1: Sk next 2 sts on last row of shirt, mark first skipped st for shorts reference, join A with sc in next st, sc in next 27 (29, 31, 33) sts, leaving rem 2 sts unworked.

Rows 2–9: Ch 1, turn, sc in each st across.

Fasten off.

FIRST AND SECOND SHOULDER

Work shoulders same as on front.
Sew shoulder seams.

Sleeves (work 2)

Rnd 1: Join A with sc in first skipped st at underarm, sc in next st, working over post of st of each row end, (sc2tog) twice, sc in each row up to last 4 rows, (sc2tog) twice, join with sl st in beg sc—22 (26, 30, 34) sc.

Rnds 2–12: Ch 1, turn, sc in each st around, join with sl st in beg sc.

Fasten off.

CUFFS

Rnd 1: Join B with sc in any st, sc in each st around, join with sl st in beg sc.

Rnds 2–5: Ch 1, turn, sc in each st around, join with sl st in beg sc.

Fasten off. Repeat on end of other sleeve.

Waistband

Rnd 1: Working in bottom loops of rnd 1 of shirt, join B with sc in any st; sc in each st around, join with sl st in beg sc—60 (64, 68, 72) sc.

Rnds 2–4: Ch 1, sc in each st around, join with sl st in beg sc.

Fasten off.

Collar

Rnd 1: Join B with sc in first skipped st on back between shoulders, sc in each skipped st; working in row ends of shoulder, sc in each row; sc in each st across second side; sc in each row of second shoulder, join with sl st in beg sc—36 (44, 52, 60) sts.

Rnd 2: Ch 1, sc in each st around, join with sl st in beg sc. Fasten off.

Shorts

Rnd 1: With RS facing, join A with sc in st aligned with st marker, sc in each st around, join with sl st in beg sc.

Rnds 2–10 (14, 18, 22): Ch 1, turn, sc in each st around, join with sl st in beg sc.

Fasten off.

First Leg

Row 1: Turn, sk first 15 (16, 17, 18) sts, join A with sc in next st, sc in next 29 (31, 33, 35) sts, leaving remaining sts unworked—30 (32, 34, 36) sc.

Rows 2–9 (9, 11, 11): Ch 1, turn, sc in each st across. Fasten off.

Second Leg

Row 1: Join A with sc in next st after first leg, sc in each st across.

Rows 2–9 (9, 11, 11): Ch 1, turn, sc in each st across. Fasten off.

Cuffs

Row 1: Join B with sc in first st, sc in each st across.

Rows 2–5: Ch 1, turn, sc in each st across.

Fasten off. Repeat on other leg.

Snap Band

Row 1: Working over row ends, join B with sc in first row on either leg of front, sc in next 12 (12, 14, 14) rows, (sc, sl st) in next row, ch 1, working in row ends of second leg, (sl st, sc) in next row, sc in each row to end.

Row 2: Ch 1, turn, sc in each st to ch-1 sp, sl st in ch-1 sp, sc in each st to end.

Fasten off. Repeat to work snap band on back.

Finishing

Sew snaps evenly spaced across snap band. Weave in ends.

HAT

With A, ch 2.

Rnd 1: Work 10 sc in 2nd ch from hook—10 sc. Place marker in last st to indicate end of rnd. Move marker up as each rnd is completed.

Rnd 2: Starting in the first sc of Rnd 1, work 2 sc in each st around—20 sc.

Rnd 3: Sc in each st around.

Rnd 4: *2 sc in next st, sc in next st; repeat from * around—30 sc.

Rnd 5: *2 sc in next st, sc in next 2 sts; repeat from * around—40 sc.

Rnds 6–7: Sc in each st around.

Rnd 8: *2 sc in next st, sc in next 3 sts; repeat from * around—50 sc.

Rnd 9: *2 sc in next st, sc in next 4 sts; repeat from * around—60 sc.

Rnd 10: Sc in each st around.

Rnd 11: *2 sc in next st, sc in next 5 sts; repeat from * around—70 sc.

Rnd 12: Sc in each st around.

Rnd 13: *Sc2tog, sc in next 5 sts; repeat from * around—60 sc.

Rnds 14–24: Sc in each st around.

Fasten off.

Brim

Rnd 1: Working in FLO, join B with sc in any st, sc in same st, sc in next 5 sts, *2 sc in next st, sc in next 5 sts; repeat from * around, join with sl st in first sc—70 sc.

Rnd 2: Ch 3, FPdc around same st as joining, FPdc around next 6 sts, *2 FPdc around next st, FPdc around next 6 sts; repeat from * around, join with sl st in top of beg ch—80 dc.

Rnd 3: Ch 3, dc in same st as joining, dc in next 3 sts, *2 dc in next st, dc in next 3 sts; repeat from * around—100 dc. Fasten off.

Finishing

Weave in ends.

Pretty as a Posy
Girl Dress and Hat

Your baby girl will be the image of spring in this sweet little dress with layered ruffles on the skirt and sleeves. The color changing is a little more advanced than that in the boy's outfit, but you won't find it difficult, as the colors simply change row by row.

YARN
Red Heart Anne Geddes Baby (80% Acrylic, 20% Nylon; 3.5 oz/100 g; 340 yd./310 m)
#591 Posy (A): 1 ball
#556 Jam (B): 1 ball

CROCHET HOOK
U.S. size F-5 (3.75 mm) or size needed to obtain gauge

ADDITIONAL MATERIALS
Stitch marker
Yarn needle

SIZES
3 (6, 9, 12) months
Note: Instructions are given for smallest size; changes for larger sizes are given in parentheses.

FINISHED MEASUREMENTS
Chest: 17¼ (18¼, 19½, 20½) in. [44 (46.5, 49.5, 52) cm]
Length: 10¾ (12¼, 13¾, 15¼) in. [27.5 (31, 35, 38.5) cm]

GAUGE
14 sc and 16 rows sc = 4 in. (10 cm)
13 dc and 8 rnds = 4 in. (10 cm)

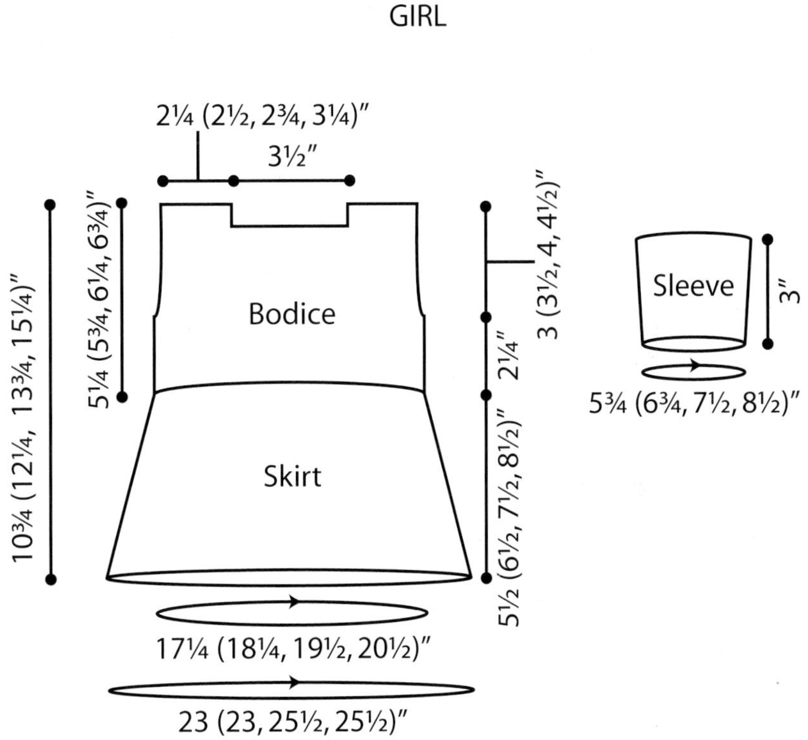

GIRL

Bodice

Skirt

Sleeve

2¼ (2½, 2¾, 3¼)"
3½"
10¾ (12¼, 13¾, 15¼)"
5¼ (5¾, 6¼, 6¾)"
3 (3½, 4, 4½)"
2¼"
5½ (6½, 7½, 8½)"
17¼ (18¼, 19½, 20½)"
23 (23, 25½, 25½)"
5¾ (6¾, 7½, 8½)"
3"

Note: Sleeves are worked directly into armholes after shoulders are seamed.

SPECIAL STITCHES
Double crochet 2 stitches together (dc2tog): [Yarn over, insert hook in next st and draw up a loop, yarn over and draw through 2 loops on hook] twice, yarn over and draw through all 3 loops on hook.

Work ruffle (worked over the surface of 2 rnds): Working around posts of sts, alternating between the two rnds, join B with sl st around any st of 1st rnd, ch 3, 2 dc around same st, sk st of 2nd rnd directly above, sc around post of next st in 2nd rnd, *sk st of 1st rnd directly below, 3 dc around post of next st in 1st rnd, sk st of 2nd rnd directly above, sc around post of next st in 2nd rnd; repeat from * around, join with sl st in top of beg ch. Fasten off.

NOTES
1. Dress is worked from waist up, split for front and back, with skirt added after. Sleeves are worked directly into armholes.
2. Ruffles are worked around sleeves and skirt after every 2 rnds. Refer to "work ruffle" instructions in the special technique section above.

DRESS

Bodice

Work same as boy shirt to sleeves.
Sew shoulder seams.

Sleeves (work 2)

Rnd 1: Join A with sl st in first skipped st at underarm, ch 3 (counts as first dc here and throughout), dc in next st; working over post of st of each row end, (dc2tog) 1 (1, 2, 2) time(s), dc in each row up to last 4 rows, (dc2tog) 1 (1, 2, 2) time(s), join with sl st in top of beg ch—24 (28, 30, 34) dc.

Rnd 2: Ch 3, dc in each st around, join with sl st in top of beg ch. Fasten off.

With B, work ruffle over last 2 rnds worked.

Rnd 3: With RS facing, join B with sl st in same st as joining, ch 3, dc in next st, (dc2tog) twice, dc in each st up to last 4 sts, (dc2tog) twice, join with sl st in top of beg ch—20 (24, 26, 30) dc.

Rnd 4: With B, repeat Rnd 2.

With A, work ruffle over last 2 rnds worked.

Rnd 5: With RS facing, join A with sl st in any st, ch 3, dc in each st around, join with sl st in top of beg ch.

Rnd 6: With A, repeat Rnd 2.

With B, work ruffle over last 2 rnds worked.
Fasten off.

Collar

Rnd 1: Join B with sc in first skipped st on last row of bodice, *sc in each st across, working over post of st of row ends, sc in each row; repeat from * around, join with sl st in beg sc. Fasten off.

Skirt

Rnd 1: Working in bottom loops of Rnd 1 of bodice, join B with sl st in any st, ch 3 (counts as dc here and throughout), dc in each st around, evenly spacing 0 (4, 0, 2) decreases (dc2tog) and 0 (0, 2, 0) increases (2 dc in one stitch) around round, join with sl st in top of beg ch—60 (60, 70, 70) dc.

Rnd 2: Ch 3, dc in each st around, join with sl st in top of beg ch. Fasten off.

With A, work ruffle over last 2 rnds worked.

Rnd 3: Join A with sl st in any st, ch 3, dc in same st, dc in next 5 (5, 6, 6) sts, *2 dc in next st, dc in next 5 (5, 6, 6) sts; repeat from * around, join with sl st in top of beg ch—70 (70, 80, 80) dc.

Rnd 4: With A, repeat Rnd 2.

With B, work ruffle over last 2 rnds worked.

Rnd 5: Join B with sl st in any st, ch 3, dc in same st, dc in next 6 (6, 7, 7) sts, *2 dc in next st, dc in next 6 (6, 7, 7) sts; repeat from * around, join with sl st in top of beg ch—80 (80, 90, 90) dc.

Rnd 6: Repeat Rnd 2.

Rnd 7: Join A with sl st in any st, ch 3, dc in same st, dc in next 7 (7, 8, 8) sts, *2 dc in next st, dc in next 7 (7, 8, 8) sts; repeat from * around, join with sl st in top of beg ch—90 (90, 100, 100) dc.

Rnd 8: Repeat Rnd 4.

With B, work ruffle over last 2 rnds worked.

Rnd 9: Join B with sl st in any st, ch 3, dc in same st, dc in next 8 (8, 9, 9) sts, *2 dc in next st, dc in next 8 (8, 9, 9) sts; repeat from * around, join with sl st in top of beg ch—100 (100, 110, 110) dc.

3 Months Only

Rnd 10: Repeat Rnd 2.

Rnd 11: Join A with sl st in any st, ch 3, dc in same st, dc in next 10 sts, *2 dc in next st, dc in next 10 sts; repeat from * around, join with sl st in top of beg ch, fasten off—110 dc.

6, 9, and 12 Months Only

Rnd 10: Repeat Rnd 2.

Rnd 11: Join A with sl st in any st, ch 3, dc in same st, dc in next 9 (10, 10) sts, *2 dc in next st, dc in next 9 (10, 10) sts; repeat from * around, join with sl st in top of beg ch—110 (120, 120) dc.

Rnd 12: Repeat Rnd 4.

With B, work ruffle over last 2 rnds worked.

Rnd 13: Join B with sl st in any st, ch 3, dc in same st, dc in next 10 (11, 11) sts, *2 dc in next st, dc in next 10 (11, 11) sts; repeat from * around, join with sl st in top of beg ch—120 (130, 130) dc.

9 Months Only

Rnd 14: Repeat Rnd 2.

Rnd 15: Join A with sl st in any st, ch 3, dc in same st, dc in next 13 sts, *2 dc in next st, dc in next 13 sts; repeat from * around, join with sl st in top of beg ch, fasten off—140 dc.

12 Months Only

Rnd 14: Repeat Rnd 2.

Rnd 15: Join A with sl st in any st, ch 3, dc in same st, dc in next 12 sts, *2 dc in next st, dc in next 12 sts; repeat from * around, join with sl st in top of beg ch—140 dc.

Rnd 16: Repeat Rnd 4.

With B, work ruffle over last 2 rnds worked.

Rnd 17: Join B with sl st in any st, ch 3, dc in same st, dc in next 13 sts, *2 dc in next st, dc in next 13 sts; repeat from * around, join with sl st in top of beg ch, fasten off—150 dc.

Finishing

Weave in ends.

HAT

Work same as boy hat through Rnd 23.

Rnds 24–25: Ch 3, dc in each st around, join with sl st in top of beg ch.

Fasten off.

With B, work ruffle over last 2 rnds worked.

Finishing

Weave in ends.

CHAPTER FIVE

May
Fly Away Home

Ladybird, ladybird, fly away home
Your house is on fire and your children are gone
All except one, and that's Little Anne
For she has crept under the warming pan.

—*Traditional children's nursery rhyme*

Many cultures around the world consider ladybugs a sign of good luck. So who could resist dressing up their baby in a cute little ladybug outfit?

Scarlet Beetle
Tank Top and Hat

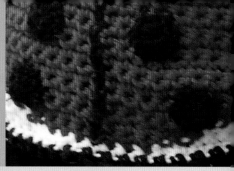

SKILL LEVEL

■■■□

INTERMEDIATE

Your darling baby will be your living good luck charm when dressed in this cute tank top and matching hat. If anyone objects to dressing baby boy as a ladybug, tell everyone your little boy is a Scarlet Beetle. A boy is just as deserving of a little bit of good luck!

YARN

Garn Studio DROPS Cotton Light (50% Cotton, 50% Polyester; 1.8 oz/50 g; 115 yd./105 m)

#02 White (A): 3 (3, 3, 3) balls
#32 Red (B): 2 (2, 2, 2) balls
#20 Black (C): 2 (2, 2, 2) balls

CROCHET HOOK

U.S. size G-6 (4 mm) or size needed to obtain gauge

ADDITIONAL MATERIALS

Yarn needle
2 stitch markers
2 Blumenthal Lansing Favorite Findings ladybug buttons
Sewing needle and matching thread

SIZES

0–3 months (3–6 months, 6–12 months, 12–18 months)
Note: Instructions are given for smallest size; changes for larger sizes are given in parentheses.

FINISHED MEASUREMENTS

Chest: 16½ (17½, 19, 20) in. (42 (44.5, 48.5, 51) cm]
Length: 11 in. (28 cm), including bottom border and straps
Note: Piece will lengthen when worn.

GAUGE

14 sc and 16 rows = 4 in. (10 cm)

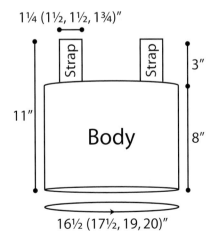

SPECIAL STITCH

Foundation single crochet (fsc): *Step 1:* Place a slip knot on hook, ch 2, insert hook in 2nd ch from hook and draw up a loop; yarn over and draw through one loop on hook (the "chain"); yarn over and draw through 2 loops on hook (the "single crochet"). *Step 2:* Insert hook into the "chain" of the previous stitch and draw up a loop, yarn over and draw through one loop on hook (the "chain"), yarn over and draw through 2 loops on hook (the "single crochet"). Repeat for the length of foundation.

NOTES

1. The top is worked in joined and turned rnds, beginning at the lower edge.

2. The ladybug pattern is worked over the center 27 sts of the front. Markers are used to indicate where to begin and end the ladybug pattern. The ladybug pattern can be worked by following the written instructions or reading the chart. Read RS rows of the chart from right to left and WS rows from left to right.

3. To change color, work last stitch of old color to last yarn over. Yarn over with new color and draw through all loops on hook to complete stitch. Proceed with new color. Carry colors not in use up back of piece until needed again.

4. The top can be lengthened a number of ways:
   • Rnd 29 can be repeated to add an extra A-colored section to the top
   • Rnds of A can be worked around lower edge before working the 2 bottom border rnds to add an extra A-colored section at the bottom
   • More rows can be worked on the straps.
   Each additional rnd of body adds about ¼ in. (6 mm) to the length. Each additional row of straps adds about ⅛ in. (3 mm) to the length.

TOP

Body

With A, fsc 58 (62, 66, 70), join with sl st to form ring.

Place a marker on the 2nd (3rd, 4th, 5th) st and the 28th (29th, 30th, 31st) st. The markers indicate where to begin and end the ladybug pattern. The first stitch of ladybug pattern should be worked in the first marked st and the last st of the ladybug pattern should be worked in the last marked st. Move the markers up as each rnd is worked.

Rnd 1 (RS): Ch 1, sc in each st to first marker; sc in next 10 sts, changing to B in last st; sc in next 3 sts, changing to C in last st; sc in next st and change to B; sc in next 3 sts, changing to A in last st; sc in each st to end of rnd, join with sl st in beg sc.

Rnd 2: Ch 1, turn, sc in each st to first marker; sc in next 8 sts, changing to B in last st; sc in next 5 sts, changing to C in last st; sc in next st and change to B; sc in next 5 sts, changing to A in last st; sc in each st to end of rnd, join with sl st in beg sc.

Rnd 3: Ch 1, turn, sc in each st to first marker; sc in next 7 sts, changing to B in last st; sc in next 6 sts, changing to C in last st; sc in next st and change to B; sc in next 6 sts, changing to A in last st; sc in each st to end of rnd, join with sl st in beg sc.

Rnd 4: Ch 1, turn, sc in each st to first marker; sc in next 6 sts, changing to B in last st; sc in next 7 sts, changing to C in last st; sc in next st and change to B; sc in next 7 sts, changing to A in last st; sc in each st to end of rnd, join with sl st in beg sc.

Rnd 5: Ch 1, turn, sc in each st to first marker; sc in next 5 sts, changing to B in last st; sc in next 8 sts, changing to C in last st; sc in next st and change to B; sc in next 8 sts, changing to A in last st; sc in each st to end of rnd, join with sl st in beg sc.

Ladybug Chart

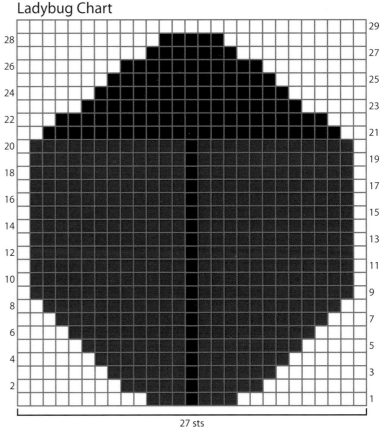

27 sts

Rnd 6: Ch 1, turn, sc in each st to first marker; sc in next 4 sts, changing to B in last st; sc in next 9 sts, changing to C in last st; sc in next st and change to B; sc in next 9 sts, changing to A in last st; sc in each st to end of rnd, join with sl st in beg sc.

Rnd 7: Ch 1, turn, sc in each st to first marker; sc in next 3 sts, changing to B in last st; sc in next 10 sts, changing to C in last st; sc in next st and change to B; sc in next 10 sts, changing to A in last st; sc in each st to end of rnd, join with sl st in beg sc.

Rnd 8: Ch 1, turn, sc in each st to first marker; sc in next 2 sts, changing to B in last st; sc in next 11 sts, changing to C in last st; sc in next st and change to B; sc in next 11 sts, changing to A in last st; sc in each st to end of rnd, join with sl st in beg sc.

Rnds 9–20: Ch 1, turn, sc in each st to first marker; sc in next st and change to B; sc in next 12 sts, changing to C in last st; sc in next st and change to B, sc in next 12 sts, changing to A in last st; sc in each st to end of rnd, join with sl st in beg sc.

Fasten off B.

Rnd 21: Ch 1, turn, sc in each st to first marker; sc in next 2 sts, changing to C in last st; sc in next 23 sts, changing to A in last st; sc in each st to end of rnd, join with sl st in beg sc.

Rnd 22: Ch 1, turn, sc in each st to first marker; sc in next 3 sts, changing to C in last st; sc in next 21 sts, changing to A in last st; sc in each st to end of rnd, join with sl st in beg sc.

Rnd 23: Ch 1, turn, sc in each st to first marker; sc in next 5 sts, changing to C in last st; sc in next 17 sts, changing to A in last st; sc in each st to end of rnd, join with sl st in beg sc.

Rnd 24: Ch 1, turn, sc in each st to first marker, sc in next 6 sts, changing to C in last st; sc in next 15 sts, changing to A in last st; sc in each st to end of rnd, join with sl st in beg sc.

Rnd 25: Ch 1, turn, sc in each st to first marker, sc in next 7 sts, changing to C in last st; sc in next 13 sts, changing to A in last st; sc in each st to end of rnd, join with sl st in beg sc.

Rnd 26: Ch 1, turn, sc in each st to first marker, sc in next 8 sts, changing to C in last st; sc in next 11 sts, changing to A in last st; sc in each st to end of rnd, join with sl st in beg sc.

Rnd 27: Ch 1, turn, sc in each st to first marker, sc in next 10 sts, changing to C in last st; sc in next 7 sts, changing to A in last st; sc in each st to end of rnd, join with sl st in beg sc.

Rnd 28: Ch 1, turn, sc in each st to first marker, sc in next 11 sts, changing to C in last st; sc in next 5 sts, changing to A in last st; sc in each st to end of rnd, join with sl st in beg sc.

Fasten off C. Remove markers.

Rnd 29: Ch 1, turn, sc in each st around, join with sl st in beg sc.

Fasten off A.

First Strap

Row 1: With RS facing, sk first 4 sts, join B with sc in next st, sc in next 3 (4, 4, 5) sts; leave remaining sts unworked—4 (5, 5, 6) sc.

Rows 2–22: Ch 1, turn, sc in each st across.

Fasten off, leaving a long tail for sewing.

Second Strap

Row 1: With RS facing, sk next 13 (13, 15, 15) sts following first strap, join B with sc in next st, sc in next 3 (4, 4, 5) sts; leave remaining sts unworked—4 (5, 5, 6) sc.

Rows 2–22: Ch 1, turn, sc in each st across.

Fasten off, leaving a long tail for sewing. With long tails, sew ends of straps to back of top, leaving 10 sts at back between ends of straps. With sewing needle and matching thread, sew one button to top of each front shoulder.

Neck Edging

Rnd 1: With RS facing, join C with sc in back neck edge near beg of one strap. Working in ends of rows and unworked sts of neck opening, sc evenly around neck edge; join with sl st in beg sc. Fasten off.

Armhole Edging

Rnd 1: With RS facing, join C with sc in armhole edge near center of underarm. Working in ends of rows and unworked sts of armhole opening, sc evenly around armhole edge; join with sl st in beg sc. Fasten off. Repeat around other armhole edge.

Bottom Border

Rnd 1: Working in bottom loops of Rnd 1 of body, join C with sl st in any st, ch 3, dc in same st, dc in each st around, join with sl st in top of beg ch. Fasten off.

Rnd 2 (Boy version): With RS facing, join B with sc in any st, sc in each st around, join with sl st in beg sc. Fasten off.

Rnd 2 (Girl version): With RS facing, join B with sl st in any st, ch 2, sc in 2nd ch from hook, *sk next st, sl st in next st, ch 2, sc in 2nd ch from hook; repeat from * around, join with sl st in same st as joining. Fasten off.

Spots (make 8)

With C, ch 2.

Rnd 1: Work 10 sc in 2nd ch from hook, join with sl st in beg sc. Fasten off, leaving a long tail for sewing.

Finishing

Following photo for placement, sew spots in place. Weave in ends.

HAT
Crown

With B, ch 8.

Row 1 (RS): Sc in 2nd ch from hook and next 2 ch, changing to C in last st; sc in next ch and change to B; sc in last 3 ch—7 sc. Place a marker in the C-colored st.

Rows 2–6: Ch 1, turn, 2 sc in first st, sc in each st to marked st, changing to C in last st; sc in next st and change to B; sc in each st to last st, 2 sc in last st—17 sc at the end of Row 6.

Rows 7–17: Ch 1, turn, sc in first 8 sts, changing to C in last st; sc in next st and change to B; sc in each st across. Fasten off B and C.

Row 18: With WS facing, join C with sl st in first st, ch 1, sc2tog, sc in each st to last 2 sts, sc2tog—15 sc.

Rows 19–23: Ch 1, turn, sc2tog, sc in each st to last 2 sts, sc2tog—5 sc at the end of row 23.

Row 24 (Edging Row): Ch 1, pivot to work over row ends, sc in end of each row across side edge; working in bottom loops of row 1, sc in each st across lower edge; sc in end of each row across other side; sl st in first st of row 23. Fasten off.

Body

Rnd 1: With RS facing, working in BLO, join A with sc in first st of Row 23, sc in each st across, sc in each st of edging, join with sl st in beg sc.

Rnd 2: Ch 3, dc in each st around, join with sl st in top of beg ch.

Fasten off.

Boy Version

Rnd 3: Working in BLO, join C with sc in any st, sc in each st around, join with sl st in beg sc.

Rnds 4–9: Ch 1, sc in each st around, join with sl st in beg sc.

Fasten off.

Girl Version

Rnd 3: Working in BLO, join B with sc in any st, sc in each st around, join with sl st in beg sc.

Rnds 4–9: Ch 1, sc in each st around, join with sl st in beg sc.

Fasten off.

Brim (Girl Version Only)

Rnd 1: With RS facing, working around post of sts, join C with sc around post of any st, sc around post of each st around, join with sl st in beg sc. Fasten off.

Rnd 2: With RS facing, join B with sl st in any st, ch 2, sc in 2nd ch from hook, *sk next st, sl st in next st, ch 2, sc in 2nd ch from hook; repeat from * around, join with sl st in same st as joining. Fasten off.

Spots (make 6)

With C, ch 2.

Rnd 1: Work 10 sc in 2nd ch from hook, join with sl st in beg sc. Fasten off, leaving a long tail for sewing.

Finishing

Following photo for placement, sew spots in place. Weave in ends.

CHAPTER SIX

June

Beach Babies

The start of summer is just the right time for your baby's first swimsuit! Beat the heat in these cute swim sets made from Cascade Fixation. The elastic fiber added to this cotton yarn makes the suits easy to put on and take off and helps keep them from sagging when wet. The sandals will protect baby's tender feet from hot sand or pavement while the adorable hat will shade your baby's delicate scalp and sensitive eyes.

Sand Crawler Boy Trunks, Hat, and Sandals

Your little boy will be all set for a day at the beach or the pool in these adorable swim trunks with vertical stripes of turquoise and moss. The trunks are designed to fit comfortably over a swim diaper so baby will have plenty of freedom to crawl around.

SKILL LEVEL

EASY

YARN
Cascade Yarns Fixation (98.3% Cotton, 1.7% Elastic;
1.76 oz/50 g; 100 yd./91 m)
#2328 Turquoise (A): 1 ball
#5800 Moss (B): 1 ball

CROCHET HOOK
U.S. size G-6 (4 mm) or size needed to obtain gauge

ADDITIONAL MATERIALS
Stitch markers
Yarn needle

SIZES
0–3 months (3–6 months, 6–12 months, 12–18 months)
Note: Instructions are given for smallest size; changes for
larger sizes are given in parentheses.

FINISHED MEASUREMENTS
Trunks
Waist: 15 (16, 17, 17½) in. [38 (40.5, 43, 44.5) cm]
Hips: 16 (17½, 19, 20½) in. [40.5 (44.5, 48.5, 52) cm]
Length: 7 (7½, 8, 8½) in. [18 (19, 20.5, 21.5) cm], including
cuff and waistband
Hat
Circumference: 15 in. (38 cm)
Height: 5 in. (12.5 cm), including brim

GAUGE
20 sc and 22 rows/rnds unstretched = 4 in. (10 cm)

NOTES
1. The yarn used here produces a stretchy fabric. All
pieces are designed to be small, with about 3 in.
(7.5 cm) of negative ease, and will stretch to fit. The
finished measurements provided are unstretched.

2. To change color, work last stitch of old color to last
yarn over. Yarn over with new color and draw through
all loops on hook to complete stitch. Proceed with
new color. Drop old color to back of work until
needed.

3. Trunks are made in 2 halves that are folded over and
seamed halfway to create the body. Each half is then
seamed together to form the legs.

BOY

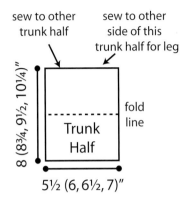

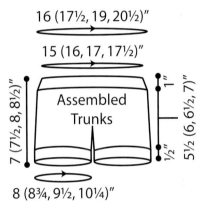

TRUNKS (make 2)
With A, ch 29 (31, 33, 35).

Row 1: Sc in 2nd ch from hook and in each ch across,
changing to B in last st—28 (30, 32, 34) sc.

Row 2: Ch 1, turn, sc in each st across.

Row 3: Ch 1, turn, sc in each st across, changing to A
in last st.

Row 4: Ch 1, turn, sc in each st across.

Row 5: Ch 1, turn, sc in each st across, changing to B
in last st.

Rows 6–41 (45, 49, 53): Repeat last 4 rows 9 (10, 11,
12) times.

Rows 42 (46, 50, 54) and 43 (47, 51, 55): Repeat Rows
2–3.

Row 44 (48, 52, 56): Ch 1, turn, sc in each st across.

Fasten off, leaving a long tail for sewing.

Assembly

Matching up sts of last row on one panel with foundation chain lps of Row 1 on second panel, using yarn needle, sew 20 (21, 22, 23) sts together, leaving remaining sts open for legs. Bring remaining ends of panels together at center, matching up sts with foundation chain lps of opposite end, and sew 20 (21, 22, 23) sts together. Matching up the remaining sts of one panel with the foundation chain lps of the same panel, sew together to form first leg. Repeat for second leg.

Waistband

Rnd 1: Working over row ends at top of body, join A with sc in edge at center front, sc in each row around, join with sl st in beg sc—88 (96, 104, 112) sts.

Rnd 2: Ch 1, sc in first 0 (4, 3, 5) sc, *sc in next 4 (3, 3, 2) sts, sc2tog; repeat from * to last 4 (7, 6, 7) sts, sc in last 4 (7, 6, 7) sts, join with sl st in beg sc—74 (79, 85, 87) sc.

Rnds 3–6: Ch 1, sc in each st around, join with sl st in beg sc.
Fasten off.

Cuff

Rnd 1: Working over row ends at bottom of leg, join A with sc in any row, sc in each row around, join with sl st in beg sc—44 (48, 52, 56) sc.

Rnds 2–3: Ch 1, sc in each st around, join with sl st in beg sc.
Fasten off. Repeat for second leg.

Finishing

Weave in ends.

HAT
Crown
With A, ch 3, join with sl st to form ring.

Rnd 1: 10 sc in ring, join with sl st in beg sc—10 sc.

> **NOTE** Work first st of each rnd in same st as joining sl st.

Rnd 2: Ch 1, 2 sc in each st around, join with sl st in beg sc—20 sc.

Rnd 3: Ch 1, sc in each st around, join with sl st in beg sc.

Rnd 4: Repeat Rnd 2—40 sc.

Rnds 5–6: Repeat Rnd 3.

Rnd 7: Ch 1, *sc in next st, 2 sc in next st; repeat from * around, join with sl st in beg sc—60 sc.

Rnd 8: Ch 1, *sc in next 5 sts, 2 sc in next st; repeat from * around, join with sl st in beg sc—70 sc.

Rnds 9–10: Repeat Rnd 3.

Fasten off.

Body
Rnd 1: Working in BLO, join B with sc in any st, sc in each st around, join with sl st in beg sc.

Rnds 2–20: Ch 1, sc in each st around, join with sl st in beg sc.

Fasten off.

Brim
Rnd 1: Ch 1, working in FLO, join A with sc in any st, sc in each st around, join with sl st in beg sc.

Rnd 2: Ch 3 (counts as first dc here and throughout), sk first st, 2 dc in next st, *dc in next st, 2 dc in next st; repeat from * around, join with sl st in top of beg ch—105 dc.

Rnd 3: Ch 3, dc in each st around, join with sl st in top of beg ch.

Fasten off.

Finishing
Weave in ends.

SANDALS (make 2)
With 2 strands of A held together, ch 11.

Rnd 1: Work 2 sc in 2nd ch from hook, sc in next 8 ch, 4 sc in last ch, working in bottom lps of starting ch, sc in next 8 ch, 2 sc in same ch as beg sc, join with sl st in beg sc—24 sc.

Rnd 2: Ch 1, 2 sc in first st, sc in next 10 sts, 2 sc in each of next 2 sts, sc in next 10 sts, 2 sc in last st, join with sl st in beg sc—28 sc.

Rnd 3: Ch 1, 3 sc in first st, sc in next 12 sts, 3 sc in each of next 2 sts, sc in next 12 sts, 3 sc in last st, join with sl st in beg sc—36 sc.

Rnd 4: Ch 1, 3 sc in first st, sc in next 16 sts, 3 sc in each of next 2 sts, sc in next 16 sts, 3 sc in last st, join with sl st in beg sc—44 sc. Fasten off.

Edging
Rnd 1: Join 1 strand of B with sl st in any st, sl st in each st around. Fasten off.

Toe Strap
With 2 strands of A held together, join yarn with sl st around post of st at center of Rnd 2 at either end, ch 10, sk 10 sts from top center, join with sl st in next st, mark this st, ch 1, sl st in each ch, sl st in same sp as joining sl st, ch 10, sk 10 sts from top center in opposite direction, join with sl st in next st, mark this st, ch 1, sl st in each ch. Fasten off.

Back Strap
With 2 strands of A held together, join yarn with sl st in either marked st, ch 11, sl st in second marked st, sc in each ch, sl st in same st as joining sl st. Fasten off.

Finishing
Weave in ends.

Tutti Frutti Girl Bikini, Hat, and Sandals

Your little girl will be ready for a day in the sun in this cute little bikini in shades of fuchsia and tangerine. The tie at the neck will keep the top secure while baby is busy playing in the sand or splashing in the water.

SKILL LEVEL

EASY

YARN
Cascade Yarns Fixation (98.3% Cotton, 1.7% Elastic;
   1.76 oz/50 g; 100 yd./91 m)
#6185 Fuchsia (A): 1 ball
#3417 Tangerine (B): 1 ball

CROCHET HOOK
U.S. size G-6 (4 mm) or size needed to obtain gauge

ADDITIONAL MATERIALS
Stitch markers
Yarn needle

SIZES
0–3 months (3–6 months, 6–12 months, 12–18 months)
Note: Instructions are given for smallest size; changes for
   larger sizes are given in parentheses.

FINISHED MEASUREMENTS
Top
Chest: 14 (14½, 15½, 16) in. [35.5 (37, 39.5, 40.5) cm]
Length: 3 in. [7.5 cm], not including edgings
Bottom
Waist/Hips: 14½ (15, 16, 17) in. [37 (38, 40.5, 43) cm]
Hat
Circumference: 15 in. (38 cm)
Height: 5 in. (12.5 cm), including ruffle

GAUGE
20 sc and 22 rows/rnds unstretched = 4 in. (10 cm)

GIRL

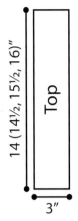

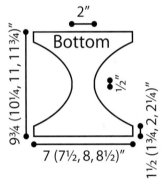

NOTES
1. The yarn used here produces a stretchy fabric. All pieces are designed to be small, with about 3 in. (7.5 cm) of negative ease, and will stretch to fit. The finished measurements provided are unstretched.
2. To change color, work last stitch of old color to last yarn over. Yarn over with new color and draw through all loops on hook to complete stitch. Proceed with new color. Drop old color to back of work until needed.
3. Bottom is worked from the waist down and then back up again and seamed together.

TOP
With A, ch 16.
Row 1: Sc in 2nd ch from hook and each ch across—15 sc.
Row 2: Ch 1, turn, sc in each st across, changing to B in last st.
Row 3: Ch 1, turn, sc in each st across.
Row 4: Ch 1, turn, sc in each st across, changing to A in last st.
Row 5: Ch 1, turn, sc in each st across.
Rows 6–73 (77, 81, 85): Repeat last 4 rows 17 (18, 19, 20) times.
Next 3 Rows: Repeat Rows 2–4, but do not change color at the end of the last row.
Fasten off, leaving a long tail for sewing. Matching up sts of last row with bottom loops of Row 1, sew seam together.

Bottom Edging and Ruffle (shaped edge)

Rnd 1: Working over row ends, join B with sc in any row, sc in each row around, join with sl st in beg sc—76 (80, 84, 88) sc.

Rnd 2: Ch 3, sl st in first st, *sk next st, (sl st, ch 3, sl st) in next st; repeat from * to last st, leave last st unworked.

Fasten off.

Top Edging

Rnd 1: Working over row ends of opposite side, join B with sc in any row, sc in each row around, join with sl st in beg sc.

Rnd 2: Ch 1, sl st in each st around.

Fasten off.

Tie

With B, ch 120, sl st in 2nd ch from hook, *ch 3, sl st in next ch; repeat from * across.

Fasten off. Fold tie in half and sew to center of front at top edging.

Finishing

Weave in ends.

BOTTOM

With A, ch 37 (39, 41, 43).

Row 1: Sc in 2nd ch from hook and each ch across— 36 (38, 40, 42) sc.

Rows 2–8 (9, 10, 11): Ch 1, turn, sc in each st across.

Decrease Row: Ch 1, turn, sc2tog, sc in each st up to last 2 sts, sc2tog—34 (36, 38, 40) sc.

Repeat decrease row 8 (9, 10, 11) more times—18 sc.

Next Row: Ch 1, turn, sc in each st across.

Next Row: Repeat decrease row—16 sc.

Next 6 Rows: Repeat last 2 rows 3 times—10 sc.

Next 3 Rows: Ch 1, turn, sc in each st across.

Increase Row: Ch 1, turn, 2 sc in first st, sc in each st up to last st, 2 sc in last st—12 sc.

Next Row: Ch 1, turn, sc in each st across.

Next 6 Rows: Repeat last 2 rows 3 times—18 sc.

Repeat increase row 9 (10, 11, 12) times—36 (38, 40, 42) sc.

Next 8 (9, 10, 11) Rows: Ch 1, turn, sc in each st across. Do not fasten off.

Edging

Row 1: Pivot to work over row ends, ch 1, sc in each row—53 (57, 61, 65) sts.

Fasten off. Repeat across other side edge.

Assembly

Fold in half. Matching up 8 (9, 10, 11) sts on front and back edging, sew side seams together. Repeat for opposite side.

Leg Shaping and Ruffle

Rnd 1: Join B with sl st in st at center of fold, sl st in each st around, join with sl st in same st as beg sl st— 37 (39, 41, 43) sts.

Rnd 2: Ch 1, working in FLO, sc in next 8 (9, 10, 11) sts, 5 dc in next 20 sts, sc in each st to end, join with sl st in beg sc.

Fasten off. Repeat for second leg.

Waistband

Rnd 1: Join B with sc in any st, sc in each st around, join with sl st in beg sc—72 (76, 80, 84) sc.

Rnd 2: Ch 3 (counts as first dc here and throughout), dc in each st around, join with sl st in top of beg ch.

Rnd 3: Ch 1, sc in each st around, join with sl st in beg sc. Fasten off.

Rnd 4: Join A with sl st in any st, ch 3, dc in each st around, join with sl st in beg sc.

NOTE You may wish to try piece on recipient before working next rnd. Work only as many decreases (sc2tog) as needed to achieve desired fit.

Rnd 5: Ch 1, *sc in next 2 sts, sc2tog; repeat from * around, join with sl st in beg sc—54 (57, 60, 63) sts. Fasten off.

HAT

Work crown and body as for boy hat, using B for crown and A for body—70 sc. Fasten off.

Ruffle

Rnd 1: Draw up a loop of B in same st as joining, ch 3, working in FLO, 4 dc in same st, 5 dc in each st around, join with sl st in top of beg ch. Fasten off.

Finishing

Weave in ends.

SANDALS (make 2)

Work same as boy sandals.

Ties (make 2)

With A, ch 91, sl st in 2nd ch from hook and each ch across. Fasten off. Weave one tie through sts of rnd 2 on front and one on back. Tie at sides.

Finishing

Weave in ends.

CHAPTER SEVEN

July
Happy Independence Day!

Celebrate your patriotic spirit and love of your country by making one of these red, white, and blue outfits for baby. The hat will protect baby's head from the strong summer sun. The cute romper and dress allow plenty of air circulation to keep little ones from over-heating on hot summer days.

Yankee Doodle Dandy Boy Romper and Hat

Your baby boy will be an impeccable Yankee Doodle Dandy in this one-piece blue romper featuring stripes of red, white, and blue at the waist and pant leg cuffs. The coordinating hat—also featuring stripes of red, white, and blue—will be just right as a finishing touch.

SKILL LEVEL

EASY

YARN

Berroco Comfort DK (50% Super Fine Nylon, 50% Super
   Fine Acrylic; 1.75 oz/50 g; 178 yd./165 m)
#2751 True Red (A): 2 balls
#2700 Chalk (B): 2 balls
#2736 Primary Blue (C): 2 balls

CROCHET HOOK

U.S. size F-5 (3.75 mm) or size needed to obtain gauge

ADDITIONAL MATERIALS

Stitch markers
Yarn needle
Sewing needle and matching thread
2 large shank buttons, Blumenthal Lansing Favorite
   Finds #483, Patriotic Stars

SIZES

0–3 months (3–6 months, 6–9 months, 9–12 months)
Note: Instructions are given for smallest size; changes
   for larger sizes are given in parentheses.

FINISHED MEASUREMENTS

Waist: 18 (19, 19½, 20) in. [45.5 (48.5, 49.5, 51) cm]
Shorts Length: 6 (6¾, 7¼, 7¾) in. [15 (17, 18.5, 19.5) cm]
Romper Length: 11¾ (13¼, 14¼, 15) in. [30 (33.5, 36, 38)
   cm], buttoned
Hat Circumference: 15 in. (38 cm)

GAUGE

16 sc and 19 rows/rounds = 4 in. (10 cm)

SPECIAL STITCHES

Front post single crochet (FPsc): Insert hook around the
post of next stitch from front to back and then to front
again, yarn over and draw up a loop, yarn over and draw
through both loops on hook.

NOTES

1. Shorts are made first from the waist down with top
   added after.
2. To change color, work last stitch of old color to last
   yarn over. Yarn over with new color and draw through
   all loops on hook to complete stitch. Proceed with
   new color. Carry colors not in use up back of piece
   until needed again.

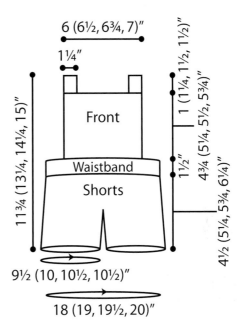

BOY

ROMPER
Waistband

With A, ch 72 (76, 78, 80), join with sl st to form ring.

Rnd 1 (RS): Sc in 2nd ch from hook and in each ch
   around, changing to B in last st; join with sl st in
   beg sc—72 (76, 78, 80) sc.

Rnd 2: Ch 1, turn, sc in each st around, changing to C
   in last st; join with sl st in beg sc.

Rnd 3: Ch 1, turn, sc in each st around, changing to A
   in last st; join with sl st in beg sc.

Rnd 4: Ch 1, turn, sc in each st around, changing to B
   in last st; join with sl st in beg sc.

Rnds 5–7: Repeat Rnds 2–4.

Rnd 8: Repeat Rnd 2.

Fasten off A and B.

Body

Work body and gusset with C only.

Rnds 1–10 (12, 13, 14): Ch 1, turn, sc in each st around,
   join with sl st in beg sc.

Fasten off.

Gusset

Row 1: With RS facing, sk next 16 (17, 17, 17) sts, join C with sc in next st, sc in next 3 (3, 4, 5) sts leaving remaining sts unworked—4 (4, 5, 6) sc.

Rows 2–6 (6, 8, 8): Ch 1, turn, sc in each st across.

Fasten off. Sk next 32 (34, 34, 34) sts; sew last row of gusset to next 4 (4, 5, 6) sts.

First Leg

Rnd 1: Join C with sc in first row of gusset; working over row ends of gusset, sc in each row end; sc in each st around leg opening, join with sl st in beg sc—38 (40, 42, 42) sc.

Rnds 2–4 (5, 6, 7): Ch 1, turn, sc in each st around, join with sl st in beg sc.

Rnd 5 (6, 7, 8): Ch 1, turn, sc in each st around, changing to A in last st, join with sl st in beg sc.

Rnd 6 (7, 8, 9): Ch 1, turn, sc in each st around, changing to B in last st, join with sl st in beg sc.

Rnd 7 (8, 9, 10): Ch 1, turn, sc in each st around, changing to C in last st, join with sl st in beg sc.

Rnds 8–10 (9–11, 10–12, 11–13): Repeat Rnds 5–7 (6–8, 7–9, 8–10).

Rnds 11–12 (12–13, 13–14, 14–15): Repeat Rnds 5–6 (6–7, 7–8, 8–9).

Fasten off.

Repeat for second leg.

Front

Row 1: With WS facing, working in bottom loops of Rnd 1, sk first 6 sts after joining, join C with sc in next st, sc in next 23 (25, 26, 27) sts, leaving remaining sts unworked—24 (26, 27, 28) sc.

Rows 2–23 (25, 26, 27): Ch 1, turn, sc in each st across.

First Shoulder

Row 1: Ch 1, turn, 2 sc in first st, sc in next 4 sts, leaving remaining sts unworked—6 sc.

Rows 2–5 (6, 7, 7): Ch 1, turn, sc in each st across.

Fasten off.

Second Shoulder

Row 1: Sk next 14 (16, 17, 18) sts on last row of front, join C with sc in next st, sc in next 3 sts, 2 sc in last st—6 sc.

Rows 2–5 (6, 7, 7): Ch 1, turn, sc in each st across.

Fasten off.

Back

Row 1: With WS facing, sk next 12 unworked bottom loops of Rnd 1 following front, join C with sc in next st, sc in next 23 (25, 26, 27) sts, leaving remaining sts unworked—24 (26, 27, 28) sc.

Rows 2–23 (25, 26, 27): Ch 1, turn, sc in each st across.

First Shoulder

Row 1: Ch 1, turn, 2 sc in first st, sc in next 4 sts, leaving remaining sts unworked—6 sc.

Rows 2–7 (8, 9, 9): Ch 1, turn, sc in each st across.

Row 8 (9, 10, 10): Ch 1, turn, sc in first 2 sts, ch 2, sk next 2 sts for buttonhole, sc in last 2 sts—4 sc, and 1 ch-2 sp.

Row 9 (10, 11, 11): Ch 1, turn, sc in each st and ch across—6 sc.

Row 10 (11, 12, 12): Ch 1, turn, sc in each st across.

Fasten off.

Second Shoulder

Row 1: Sk next 14 (16, 17, 18) sts on last row of back, join C with sc in next st, sc in next 3 sts, 2 sc in last st—6 sc.

Rows 2–10 (11, 12, 12): Work same as rows 2–10 (11, 12, 12) of first shoulder.

Fasten off.

Finishing

Weave in ends. Sew one button to each front shoulder opposite buttonhole.

HAT
Crown
With 2 strands of A held together, ch 2.

Rnd 1 (RS): 10 sc in 2nd ch from hook, join with sl st in beg sc—10 sc.

Rnd 2: Ch 1, 2 sc in next st and in each st around, join with sl st in beg sc—20 sc.

Rnd 3: Ch 1, sc in next st and in each st around, join with sl st in beg sc.

Rnd 4: Ch 1, *2 sc in next st, sc in next st; repeat from * around, join with sl st in beg sc—30 sc.

Rnd 5: Ch 1, *2 sc in next st, sc in next 2 sts; repeat from * around, join with sl st in beg sc—40 sc.

Rnd 6: Repeat Rnd 3.

Rnd 7: Ch 1, *2 sc in next st, sc in next 3 sts; repeat from * around, join with sl st in beg sc—50 sc.

Rnd 8: Repeat Rnd 3.

Rnd 9: Ch 1, *2 sc in next st, sc in next 4 sts; repeat from * around, join with sl st in beg sc—60 sc.

Rnd 10: Repeat Rnd 3.

Rnd 11: Ch 1, *2 sc in next st, sc in next 5 sts; repeat from * around, join with sl st in beg sc—70 sc.

Fasten off.

Body
Rnd 1: With RS facing and working in BLO, join B with sc in any st, sc in next 4 sts, sc2tog, *sc in next 5 sts, sc2tog; repeat from * around, join with sl st in beg sc—60 sc.

Rnds 2–3: Ch 1, sc in next st and in each st around, join with sl st in beg sc.

Fasten off.

Rnd 4: With RS facing, join C with sc in any st, sc in each st around, join with sl st in beg sc.

Rnds 5–6: Repeat Rnds 2–3.

Fasten off B and join A.

Rnds 7–9: With A, repeat Rnds 4–6.

Rnds 10–12: With B, repeat Rnds 4–6.

Rnds 13–15: Repeat Rnds 4–6.

Fasten off.

Brim

Rnd 1: Working around posts of sts, with RS facing, join A with sc around any st, ch 1, sk next st, *FPsc around next st, ch 1, sk next st; repeat from * around, join with sl st in beg sc—30 sc and 30 ch-1 sp.

Rnd 2: Ch 2 (counts as hdc), working over ch-1 and in skipped sts of previous rnd, 2 dc in next skipped st, *hdc in next sc, 2 dc in next skipped st; repeat from * around, join with sl st in top of beg ch.

Rnd 3: Ch 3, dc in each st around, join with sl st in top of beg ch. Fasten off.

Finishing

Weave in ends.

Lady Liberty Girl
Dress and Hat

The shell stitch pattern adds a very feminine touch to the red, white, and blue stripes of the hat and the skirt of this A-line tank dress. The red tie at the waist makes this dress adjustable, which means your baby will be able to wear it as a tank top as she grows.

YARN

Berroco Comfort DK (50% Super Fine Nylon, 50% Super
Fine Acrylic; 1.75 oz/50 g; 178 yd./165 m)
#2751 True Red (A): 2 balls
#2700 Chalk (B): 2 balls
#2736 Primary Blue (C): 2 balls

CROCHET HOOK

U.S. size F-5 (3.75 mm) or size needed to obtain gauge

ADDITIONAL MATERIALS

Stitch markers
Yarn needle
Sewing needle and matching thread
2 small shank buttons, Blumenthal Lansing Favorite
Finds #483, Patriotic Stars

SIZES

0–3 months (3–6 months, 6–9 months, 9–12 months)
Note: Instructions are given for smallest size; changes
for larger sizes are given in parentheses.

FINISHED MEASUREMENTS

Waist: 16 (17¼, 18¾, 20) in. [40.5 (44, 47.5, 51) cm]
Skirt Length: 9 (9, 10¼, 10¼) in. [23 (23, 26, 26) cm]
Dress Length: 13½ (14¼ 16, 16) in. [34.5 (36, 40.5, 40.5) cm]
Hat Circumference: 15 in. (38 cm)

GAUGE

3 pattern repeats of shell pattern = 4 in. (10 cm)
Note: One pattern repeat consists of one shell and the
following sc.
10 rounds of shell pattern = 4¼ in. (11 cm)
16 sc and 19 rows = 4 in. (10 cm)

SPECIAL STITCH

Shell: 5 dc in indicated st

NOTES

1. To change color, work last stitch of old color to last
   yarn over. Yarn over with new color and draw through
   all loops on hook to complete stitch. Proceed with
   new color. Carry colors not in use up back of piece
   until needed again.
2. The skirt of the dress is made first from the waist
   down with top added after.
3. The first shell is worked in the last sc of the previous
   rnd on the skirt and hat.

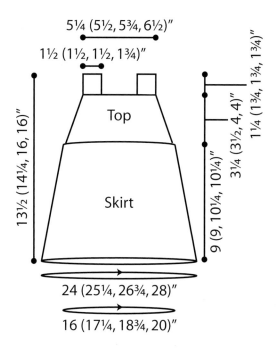

GIRL

5¼ (5½, 5¾, 6½)"

1½ (1½, 1½, 1¾)"

Top

Skirt

13½ (14¼, 16, 16)"

9 (9, 10¼, 10¼)"

3¼ (3½, 4, 4)"

1¼ (1¾, 1¾, 1¾)"

24 (25¼, 26¾, 28)"

16 (17¼, 18¾, 20)"

DRESS
Skirt

With A, ch 72 (78, 84, 90), join with sl st to form ring.

Rnd 1 (RS): Ch 1, sc in first ch, sk next 2 ch, shell in next
ch, sk next 2 ch, *sc in next ch, sk next 2 ch, shell in
next ch, sk next 2 ch; repeat from * around, join with
sl st in beg sc—12 (13, 14, 15) shells and 12 (13, 14,
15) sc (12 [13, 14, 15] pattern repeats).

Rnd 2: With RS facing, draw up a loop of B in first sc of
Rnd 1, ch 3, 4 dc in same st, sc in BLO of center st of
next shell, *shell in next sc, sc in BLO of center st of
next shell; repeat from * around, join with sl st in top
of beg ch.

Rnd 3: With RS facing, draw up a loop of C in last sc, ch
3, 4 dc in same st, sc in BLO of center st of next shell,
*shell in next sc, sc in BLO of center st of next shell;
repeat from * around, join with sl st in top of beg ch.

Rnd 4: Draw up a loop of A in last sc, ch 3, 4 dc in same
st, sc in BLO of center st of next shell, *shell in next sc,
sc in BLO of center st of next shell; repeat from *
around, join with sl st in top of beg ch.

Rnd 5: With B, repeat Rnd 4.

Rnd 6: With C, repeat Rnd 4.

Place markers in the center st of the 1st (1st, 1st, 1st), 5th (5th, 5th, 6th), and 9th (9th, 10th, 11th) shells. Move markers up as each rnd is worked.

Rnd 7: Draw up a loop of A in last sc, ch 3, 4 dc in same st, 3 sc in BLO of center st (marked) of next shell, [shell in next sc, *sc in BLO of center st of next shell, shell in next sc; repeat from * to next marked shell, 3 sc in BLO of center st of next shell] twice, **shell in next sc, sc in BLO of center st of next shell; repeat from ** around; join with sl st in top of beg ch—12 (13, 14, 15) shells and 18 (19, 20, 21) sc.

Rnd 8: Draw up a loop of B in last sc, ch 3, 4 dc in same st, sc in BLO of center st of next shell, shell in next sc, sc in next marked st, shell in next sc, [*sc in BLO of center st of next shell, shell in next sc; repeat from * to next marked sc, sc in marked sc, shell in next sc] twice, sc in BLO of center st of next shell, **shell in next sc, sc in BLO of center st of next shell; repeat from ** around; join with sl st in top of beg ch—15 (16, 17, 18) shells and 15 (16, 17, 18) sc. Remove markers.

Rnd 9: With C, repeat Rnd 4.

Rnds 10–15: Repeat Rnds 4–6 twice.

Place markers in the center st of the 1st (1st, 1st, 1st), 6th (6th, 6th, 7th), and 11th (11th, 12th, 13th) shells.

Rnds 16–21 (21, 24, 24): Repeat Rnds 7–12 (12, 15, 15)—18 (19, 20, 21) shells.

Fasten off.

Top
Front
Row 1: With RS facing, working in bottom loops of foundation chain of skirt, join C with sc in any st, sc in next 34 (37, 40, 43) sts, leaving rem sts unworked—35 (38, 41, 44) sc.

Row 2: Ch 1, turn, sc2tog, sc in each st up to last 2 sts, sc2tog—33 (36, 39, 42) sc.

Row 3: Ch 1, turn, sc in each st across.

Rows 4–15 (17, 19, 19): Repeat last 2 rows 6 (7, 8, 8) times—21 (22, 23, 26) sc.

First Shoulder
Row 1 (WS): Ch 1, turn, sc in first 8 (9, 9, 10) sts, leaving rem sts unworked—8 (9, 9, 10) sc.

Row 2: Ch 1, turn, sc in each st across.

Row 3: Ch 1, turn, sc in each st to last 2 sts, sc2tog—7 (8, 8, 9) sc.

Row 4: Ch 1, turn, sc in each st across.

Rows 5–6 (8, 8, 8): Repeat last 2 rows 1 (2, 2, 2) more time(s)—6 (6, 6, 7) sc.

Fasten off.

Second Shoulder
Row 1: With WS facing, sk next 5 (4, 5, 6) sts, join C with sc in next st, sc in next 7 (8, 8, 9) sts—8 (9, 9, 10) sc.

Row 2: Ch 1, turn, sc in each st across.

Row 3: Ch 1, turn, sc2tog, sc in each st across—7 (8, 8, 9) sc.

Row 4: Ch 1, turn, sc in each st across.

Rows 5–6 (8, 8, 8): Repeat last 2 rows 1 (2, 2, 2) more time(s)—6 (6, 6, 7) sc.

Fasten off.

Back
Row 1: With RS facing, working in bottom loops of Rnd 1, sk next st, join C with sc in next st, sc in next 34 (37, 40, 43) sts, leaving last st unworked—35 (38, 41, 44) sc.

Rows 2–15 (17, 19, 19): Work rows 2–15 (17, 19, 19) of front.

Shoulders
Work back shoulders same as front shoulders.

Finishing
Sew shoulder seams. Using photo as a guide for placement, sew buttons to the center front of the top.

Armhole Edging
Rnd 1: With RS facing, join C with sc in skipped st at underarm, sc evenly spaced around armhole edge; join with sl st in beg sc. Fasten off. Repeat for second armhole.

Neck Edging
Rnd 1: With RS facing, join C with sc anywhere in back neck edge, sc evenly spaced around neck edge; join with sl st in beg sc. Fasten off.

Ties (make 2)
With A, ch 101, sl st in 2nd ch from hook and each ch across. Fasten off.

Weave one tie through sts of row 3 (5, 7, 7) on front and one tie through sts of row 3 (5, 7, 7) on back. Tie at sides.

HAT
Crown and Body

With A, ch 3, join with sl st to form ring.

Rnd 1 (RS): Ch 3 (counts as dc here and throughout), 15 dc in ring, changing to B in last st, join with sl st in top of beg ch—16 dc.

Rnd 2: Ch 1, sc in same st as joining, 3 dc in next st, *sc in next st, 3 dc in next st; repeat from * around, changing to C in last st, join with sl st in beg sc—8 sc and 24 dc.

Rnd 3: Ch 3, 4 dc in same st as joining, sc in BLO of center st of next 3-st group, *shell in next sc, sc in BLO of center st of next 3-st group; repeat from * around, join with sl st in top of beg ch—8 shells and 8 sc.

Rnd 4: Draw up a loop of A in last sc, ch 3, 4 dc in same sc, sc in BLO of center st of next shell, *shell in next sc, sc in BLO of center st of next shell; repeat from * around, join with sl st in top of beg ch.

Rnd 5: Draw up a loop of B in last sc, ch 3, 4 dc in same sc, *3 sc in BLO of center st of next shell, shell in next sc, sc in BLO of center st of next shell, shell in next sc; repeat from * 2 more times, 3 sc in BLO of center st of next shell, shell in next sc, sc in BLO of center st of next shell, join with sl st in top of beg ch—8 shells, 16 sc.

Rnd 6: Draw up a loop of C in last sc, ch 3, 4 dc in same sc, sc in BLO of center st of next shell, *shell in next sc, sc in next sc, shell in next sc, sc in BLO of center st of next shell, shell in next sc, sc in BLO of center st of next shell; repeat from * 2 more times, shell in next sc, sc in next sc, shell in next sc, sc in BLO of center st of next shell, join with sl st in top of beg ch—12 shells and 12 sc.

Rnd 7: Draw up a loop of A in last sc, ch 3, 4 dc in same sc, sc in BLO of center st of next shell, *shell in next sc, sc in BLO of center st of next shell; repeat from * around, join with sl st in top of beg ch.

Rnd 8: Draw up a loop of B in last sc, ch 3, 4 dc in same sc, sc in BLO of center st of next shell, *shell in next sc, sc in BLO of center st of next shell; repeat from * around join with sl st in top of beg ch.

Rnd 9: Draw up a loop of C in last sc, ch 3, 4 dc in same st, sc in BLO of center st of next shell, *shell in next sc, sc in BLO of center st of next shell; repeat from * around, join with sl st in top of beg ch.

Rnds 10–15: Repeat Rnds 7–9 twice.

Rnd 16: Repeat Rnd 7.

Brim

Rnd 1: Draw up a loop of C in last sc, ch 3, 6 dc in same sc, sl st around post of center st of next shell, *7 dc around post of next sc, sl st around post of center st of next shell; repeat from * around, join with sl st in top of beg ch.

Rnd 2: Ch 3, dc in next 2 dc, 3 dc in next dc, dc in next 3 dc, sl st around same post as corresponding sl st of prev rnd, *dc in next 3 dc, 3 dc in next dc, dc in next 3 dc, sl st in same sp as previous sl st; repeat from * around, join with sl st in top of beg ch. Fasten off.

Finishing

Weave in ends.

CHAPTER EIGHT

August

Lazy Days Of Summer

Babies don't need to wear a lot of clothes in the hot summer months. These cute outfits are made from cotton yarn for comfort and breathability to keep baby from getting over-heated. Even when it's hot outside, it's still a good idea to protect baby's delicate head with a hat—not to mention they just look so darn cute.

Goldenrod Tank and Hat

This yellow and white striped tank top will keep your little man comfy and cool when worn over a pair of shorts or even just a diaper during the long, hot days of summer. The deep armholes give baby plenty of range of motion to crawl and play.

YARN
Tahki Stacy Charles Cotton Classic; (100% Mercerized
    Cotton; 1.75 oz/50 g; 108 yd./100 m)
#3001 White (A): 2 hanks
#3548 Butter Yellow (B): 2 hanks

CROCHET HOOK
U.S. size F-5 (3.75 mm) or size needed to obtain gauge

ADDITIONAL MATERIALS
Stitch marker
Yarn needle

SIZES
0–3 months (3–6 months, 6–9 months, 9–12 months)
Note: Instructions are given for smallest size; changes
    for larger sizes are given in parentheses.

FINISHED MEASUREMENTS
Chest: 17 (18, 18½, 19) in. [43 (45.5, 47, 48.5) cm]
Length: 8 (8½, 9, 9½) in. [20.5 (21.5, 23, 24) cm],
    including straps and not including ribbing

GAUGE
15 sc and 20 rows/rnds = 4 in. (10 cm)

SPECIAL STITCHES

Back post half double crochet (BPhdc): Yarn over, insert
    hook around post of next stitch from back to front
    and then to back again, yarn over and draw up loop,
    yarn over and draw through all 3 loops on hook
Front post half double crochet (FPhdc): Yarn over, insert
    hook around post of next stitch from front to back
    and then to front again, yarn over and draw up loop,
    yarn over and draw through all 3 loops on hook.

NOTES

To change color, work last stitch of old color to last
yarn over. Yarn over with new color and draw through
all loops on hook to complete stitch. Proceed with
new color. Carry colors not in use up back of piece
until needed again.

BOY

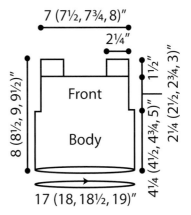

TANK TOP
Body
With A, ch 64 (68, 70, 72), join with sl st to form ring.
Rnd 1 (RS): With A, ch 1, sc in each ch around, join with
    sl st in beg sc—64 (68, 70, 72) sc.
Rnd 2: With A, ch 1, turn, sc in each st around, changing
    to B in last st, join with sl st in beg sc.
Rnd 3: With B, ch 1, turn, sc in each st around, join with
    sl st in beg sc.
Rnd 4: With B, ch 1, turn, sc in each st around, changing
    to A in last st, join with sl st in beg sc.
Rnd 5: With A, ch 1, turn, sc in each st around, join with
    sl st in beg sc.
Rnds 6–21 (23, 24, 25): Repeat last rnd, continuing to
    change color every other rnd until a total of 21 (23,
    24, 25) rnds have been worked.

Front
Continue to change color at the end of every other row
    throughout front, back, and straps.
Row 1: Ch 1, turn, sl st in next 4 sts, ch 1, sc in same st
    as last sl st made, sc in next 25 (27, 28, 29) sts, leav-
    ing remaining sts unworked—26 (28, 29, 30) sc.
Rows 2–11 (13, 14, 15): Ch 1, turn, sc in each st across.

First Strap

Row 1: Ch 1, sc in first 8 sts, leaving remaining sts unworked—8 sc.

Rows 2–7: Ch 1, turn, sc in each st across.

Fasten off.

Second Strap

Row 1: With RS facing, sk next 10 (12, 13, 14) sts on last row of front, join yarn with sc in next st, sc in next 7 sts.

Rows 2–7: Ch 1, turn, sc in each st across.

Back

Row 1: With RS facing, sk next 6 unworked sts on last row of body (for armhole), join yarn with sc in next st, sc in next 25 (27, 28, 29) sts, leaving remaining sts unworked—26 (28, 29, 30) sts.

Rows 2–11 (13, 14, 15): Ch 1, turn, sc in each st across.

Back Straps

Work both straps same as straps on front.

Finishing

Matching up sts of last row of straps, sew shoulder seam together.

Armhole Ribbing

Rnd 1: With RS facing, join B with sc in first unworked st at underarm, sc in each st; working over posts of sts at row ends, hdc in each row; join with sl st in beg sc.

Rnd 2: Ch 1, sl st in next 5 sts, FPhdc around next st, *BPhdc around next st, FPhdc around next st; repeat from * to end. Fasten off.

Repeat for second armhole.

Neck Ribbing

Rnd 1: With RS facing, join yarn with sc in first unworked st on last row of back, *sc in each st across; working over posts of sts at row ends, hdc in each row; repeat from * around, join with sl st in beg sc.

Rnd 2: *Sc in each sc, FPhdc around next hdc, [BPhdc around next hdc, FPhdc around next hdc] up to next sc; repeat from * around, join with sl st in first sc. Fasten off.

Bottom Ribbing

Rnd 1: With RS facing, working in bottom loops of Rnd 1 of body, join B with sl st in any st, ch 2 (counts as hdc), hdc in each st around, join with sl st in top of beg ch.

Rnds 2–3: Ch 2, FPhdc around next st, *BPhdc around next st, FPhdc around next st; repeat from * around, join with sl st in top of beg ch.

Fasten off.

Finishing

Weave in ends.

BEANIE

Rnd 1: With A, ch 2, 10 sc in 2nd ch from hook, mark last st—10 sc.

Use marker to keep track of ends of rnds, moving marker up as each rnd is completed.

Rnd 2: 2 sc in each st around, changing to B in last st—20 sc.

Rnd 3: Sc in each st around.

Rnd 4: *2 sc in first st, sc in next st; repeat from * around, changing to A in last st—30 sc.

Rnd 5: *2 sc in first st, sc in next 2 sts; repeat from * around—40 sc.

Rnd 6: Sc in each st around, changing to B in last st.

Rnd 7: Repeat Rnd 3.

Rnd 8: *2 sc in first st, sc in next 3 sts; repeat from * around, changing to A in last st—50 sc.

Rnd 9: *2 sc in first st, sc in next 4 sts; repeat from * around—60 sc.

Rnd 10: *2 sc in first st, sc in next 5 sts; repeat from * around, changing to B in last st—70 sc.

Continue to change color at the end of every other rnd throughout rest of hat.

Rnds 11–22: Sc in each st around.

Rnd 23: *Sc2tog, sc in next 5 sts; repeat from * around—60 sc.

Rnds 24–28: Sc in each st around.

Fasten off after last round.

Finishing

Weave in ends. Roll up last 6 rounds to create brim.

Sweet as a Daisy Girl Top and Bonnet

SKILL LEVEL

■■□□

EASY

The lacy skirting and an open back with crossed ties make this little tank dress the ideal choice for an outing on a hot summer day. The darling bonnet with the white scalloped trim will make your baby girl as pretty as a posy.

YARN
Tahki Stacy Charles Cotton Classic; (100% Mercerized
    Cotton; 1.75 oz/50 g; 108 yd./100 m)
#3001 White (A): 2 hanks
#3548 Butter Yellow (B): 3 hanks

CROCHET HOOK
U.S. size F-5 (3.75 mm) or size needed to obtain gauge

ADDITIONAL MATERIALS
Stitch marker
Yarn needle
2 buttons, Blumenthal Lansing Favorite Findings, Crazy Daisy

SIZES
0–3 months (3–6 months, 6–9 months, 9–12 months)
Note: Instructions are given for smallest size; changes for
    larger sizes are given in parentheses.

FINISHED MEASUREMENTS
Chest: 17 (18, 18½, 19) in. [43 (45.5, 47, 48.5) cm]
Length: 7¼ (7¾, 8½, 8¾) in. [18.5 (19.5, 21.5, 22) cm],
    including skirting and not including straps

GAUGE
15 sc and 20 rows/rnds = 4 in. (10 cm)
4 pattern repeats and 12 rows = 4 in. (10 cm) in lace pattern
Note: One pattern repeat consists of one (dc, ch 2, dc) and the
    following sc.

NOTES
To change color, work last stitch of old color to last yarn
over. Yarn over with new color and draw through all
loops on hook to complete stitch. Proceed with new
color. Carry colors not in use up back of piece until
needed again.

GIRL

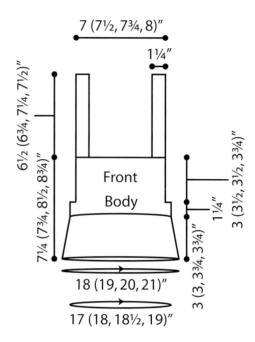

TOP
Body
With A, ch 64 (68, 70, 72), join with sl st to form ring.

Rnd 1 (RS): With A, ch 1, sc in each ch around, join with
    sl st in beg sc—64 (68, 70, 72) sc.

Rnd 2: With A, ch 1, turn, sc in each st around, changing
    to B in last st, join with sl st in beg sc.

Rnd 3: With B, ch 1, turn, sc in each st around, join with
    sl st in beg sc.

Rnd 4: With B, ch 1, turn, sc in each st around, changing
    to A in last st, join with sl st in beg sc.

Rnd 5: With A, ch 1, turn, sc in each st around, join with
    sl st in beg sc.

Rnd 6: With A, ch 1, turn, sc in each st around, changing
    to B in last st, join with sl st in beg sc.

Front

Continue to change color at the end of every other row throughout front and straps.

Row 1: Ch 1, turn, sl st in next 4 sts, ch 1, sc in same st as last sl st made, sc in next 25 (27, 28, 29) sts, leaving remaining sts unworked—26 (28, 29, 30) sc.

Rows 2–15 (17, 18, 19): Ch 1, turn, sc in each st across.

First Strap

Row 1: Ch 1, turn, sc in first 5 sts, leaving remaining sts unworked—5 sc.

Rows 2–32 (34, 36, 38): Ch 1, turn, sc in each st across. Fasten off.

Second Strap

Row 1: With RS facing, sk next 16 (18, 19, 20) sts on last row of front, join yarn with sc in next st, sc in next 4 sts.

Rows 2–32 (34, 36, 38): Ch 1, turn, sc in each st across. Fasten off.

Strap and Back Edging

Rnd 1: With RS facing, working over posts of sts at row ends, join A with sc in last row of a strap to work down outer edge of strap and side edge of front; sc in each row of strap and front; working in unworked sts across back edge, [sc in next 10 (11, 11, 11) sts, ch 2, sk next 4 sts for buttonhole] twice, sc in next 7 (7, 8, 9) sts; working over sl sts, sc in last 3 sts; sc in each row end across outer edge of other strap; working in sts of last row of strap, 2 sc in first st, sc in next 3 sts, 2 sc in last st; sc in each row end across inner edge of strap, sc in each unworked st across last row of front, sc in each row end across inner edge of other strap; working in sts of last row of strap, 2 sc in first st, sc in next 3 sts, 2 sc in last st; join with sl st in beg sc.

Rnd 2: Ch 1, loosely sl st in each st down outer edge of strap, sc in each st and ch across back, loosely sl st in each st around; join with sl st in beg sl st. Fasten off.

Skirting

Rnd 1: With RS facing, working in bottom loops of Rnd 1 of body, join B with sc in any st; sc in each st around, working 0 (0, 2, 4) increases (2 sc in same st) evenly spaced around round; join with sl st in beg sc—64 (68, 72, 76) sc.

Rnd 2: Ch 1, sc in first st, sk next st, (dc, ch 2, dc) in next st, sk next st, *sc in next st, sk next st, (dc, ch 2, dc) in next st, sk next st; repeat from * around, join with sl st in beg sc—16 (17, 18, 19) sc, 16 (17, 18, 19) ch-2 sps.

Rnd 3: Ch 5 (counts as dc, ch 2, here and throughout), dc in same st as joining, sc in next ch-2 sp, *(dc, ch 2, dc) in next sc, sc in next ch-2 sp; repeat from * around, join with slip st in 3rd ch of beg ch-5.

Rnd 4: (Sl st, ch 1, sc) in first ch-2 sp, (dc, ch 2, dc) in next sc, *sc in next ch-2 sp, (dc, ch 2, dc) in next sc; repeat from * around, join with sl st in beg sc.

Rnds 5–6 (6, 8, 8): Repeat last 2 rnds 1 (1, 2, 2) more time(s).

Next Rnd: Ch 5, (dc, [ch 2, dc] twice) in same sp as joining, [sc in next ch-2 sp, (dc, ch 2, dc) in next sc] 7 (7, 8, 8) times, (dc, [ch 2, dc] 3 times) in next sc, mark center ch-2 sp of group just made, sc in next ch-2 sp, *(dc, ch 2, dc) in next sc, sc in next ch-2 sp; repeat from * around, join with sl st in 3rd ch of beg ch-5—16 (17, 18, 19) sc and 20 (21, 22, 23) ch-2 sps.

Next Rnd: (Sl st, ch 1, sc) in first ch-2 sp, (dc, ch 2, dc) in next ch-2 sp, sc in next ch-2 sp, *(dc, ch 2, dc) in next sc, sc in next ch-2 sp; repeat from * to marked ch-2 sp, (dc, ch 2, dc) in marked ch-2 sp, **sc in next ch-2 sp, (dc, ch 2, dc) in next sc; repeat from ** around, join with sl st in beg sc—18 (19, 20, 22) sc and 18 (19, 20, 22) ch-2 sps. Fasten off.

Next Rnd: With RS facing, join A with sl st in any sc, ch 3, 4 dc in same st, sl st in next ch-2 sp, *5 dc in next sc, sl st in next ch-2 sp; repeat from * around, join with sl st in top of beg ch. Fasten off.

Finishing

Weave in ends. With RS facing, sew a button to the bottom of each strap. Cross straps over back, buttoning each in the opposite buttonhole.

BONNET

With B, ch 13.

Row 1: Sc in 2nd ch from hook and in each ch across—
12 sc.

Rows 2–9: Ch 1, turn, sc in each st across.

Row 10: Ch 1, turn, 2 sc in first st, sc in each st across—
13 sc.

Rows 11–15: Ch 1, turn, sc in each st across.

Row 16: Repeat Row 10—14 sc.

Row 17: Ch 1, turn, sc in each st across.

Row 18: Repeat Row 10—15 sc.

Rows 19–45: Ch 1, turn, sc in each st across.

Row 46: Ch 1, turn, sc2tog, sc in each st across—14 sc.

Row 47: Ch 1, turn, sc in each st across.

Row 48: Repeat Row 46—13 sc.

Rows 49–53: Ch 1, turn, sc in each st across.

Row 54: Repeat Row 46—12 sc.

Rows 55–64: Ch 1, turn, sc in each st across.
Fasten off.

Edging

Working over row ends of straight edge (this is the back
edge of the bonnet), join B with sc in first row, sc in
each row across. Fasten off.

Note: The curved edge is the front edge of the bonnet.

Back

With B, ch 3, join with sl st to form ring.

Rnd 1: Ch 1, 10 sc in ring, join with sl st in beg sc—
10 sc.

Rnd 2: Ch 1, *2 sc in next st, sc in next st; repeat from
* around, join with sl st in beg sc—20 sc.

Rnd 3: Ch 1, sc in each st around, join with sl st in
beg sc.

Rnd 4: Ch 1, *2 sc in next st, sc in next 2 sts; repeat
from * around, join with sl st in beg sc—30 sc.

Rnd 5: Ch 1, *2 sc in next st, sc in next 3 sts; repeat
from * around, join with sl st in beg sc—40 sc.

Rnd 6: Ch 1, sc in each st around, join with sl st in
beg sc.

Rnd 7: Ch 1, *2 sc in next st, sc in next 4 sts; repeat
from * around, join with sl st in beg sc—50 sc.

Rnd 8: Ch 1, sc in each st around, join with sl st in
beg sc.

Rnd 9: Ch 1, *2 sc in next st, sc in next 5 sts; repeat
from * around, join with sl st in beg sc—60 sc.

Rnd 10: Ch 1, 2 sc in first st, sc in next 29 sts, 2 sc
in next st, sc in each st around, join with sl st in
beg sc—62 sc.

Rnd 11: Ch 1, sc in each st around, join with sl st in
beg sc. Fasten off.

Assembly

With RS facing together, match up sts of edging with
last rnd of back and whipstitch together.

Ties

Join B with sl st in one front corner of bonnet, ch 50 to
create base ch for first tie. Fasten off.

Begin second tie and complete first tie: With B, ch 51,
sc in 2nd ch from hook and each ch across, sc in other
front corner of bonnet (opposite base chain of first
tie); working in ends of rows across front edge, sc in
each row across, then sc in each ch of first tie base
chain.

Row 2: Ch 1, turn, sk first st, loosely sl st in next 51 sts,
[sc2tog] 31 times, mark last st just made, loosely sl st
in each st to end. Fasten off.

Brim

Row 1: Join A with sc in marked st, *(dc, ch 2, dc) in
next st, sc in next st; repeat from * 15 times.

Row 2: Ch 1, turn, sl st in first st, *(dc, ch 3, dc) in next
ch-2 sp, sl st in next sc; repeat from * across.
Fasten off.

Finishing

Weave in ends.

September

Are You Ready for Some Football?

September means the start of the football season. Every football fan will want to dress up their little one in the colors of their favorite football team. The colors chosen here represent the Pittsburgh Steelers in memory of my dad, who was a huge fan of the team, but feel free to make these outfits in the colors of your favorite team.

Game Changer Boy Jersey, Hat, and Booties

Give your little guy an early start at becoming a game changer by dressing him in this cute little oufit for his first football game. The team jersey is accompanied by a hat and slippers that look like little footballs.

YARN

Plymouth Yarn Cleo (100% Mercerized Pima Cotton; 1.75 oz/50 g; 125 yd./114 m)
#0106 Lemon (A): 3 hanks
#0500 Black (B): 2 hanks
#0117 Russet (C): 2 hanks
#0101 Cream (D): 1 hank

CROCHET HOOK

U.S. size F-5 (3.75 mm) or size needed to obtain gauge

ADDITIONAL MATERIALS

Stitch markers
Yarn needle

SIZES

3 (6, 9, 12) months
Note: Instructions are given for smallest size; changes for larger sizes are given in parentheses.

FINISHED MEASUREMENTS

Jersey Chest: 17 (18, 19, 20) in. [43 (45.5, 48.5, 51) cm]
Jersey Length: 7¼ (8¼, 9½, 10½) in. [18.5 (21, 24, 26.5) cm]
Hat Circumference: 15 in. (38 cm)

GAUGE

16 sc and 20 rows/rnds = 4 in. (10 cm)

NOTES

1. Jersey is worked in rnds from bottom up to armholes. Front and back are split and worked in rows up to shoulders. Sleeves are worked directly into armholes.
2. Do not turn when working in rounds with color B.

JERSEY

Body

With A, ch 68 (72, 76, 80), join with sl st to form ring.

Rnd 1 (RS): Ch 1, sc in each ch around, join with sl st in beg sc—68 (72, 76, 80) sc.

Rnds 2–5: Ch 1, turn, sc in each st around, join with sl st in beg sc.

Fasten off.

Rnd 6: With RS facing, join B with sc in any st, sc in each st around, join with sl st in beg sc.

Rnd 7: Ch 1, do not turn, sc in each st around, join with sl st in beg sc. Fasten off.

BOY

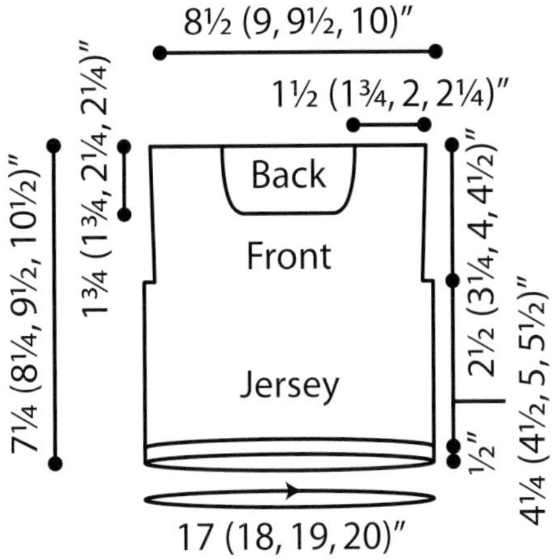
8½ (9, 9½, 10)"
1½ (1¾, 2, 2¼)"
Back
Front
Jersey
7¼ (8¼, 9½, 10½)"
1¾ (1¾, 2¼, 2¼)"
2½ (3¼, 4, 4½)"
4¼ (4½, 5, 5½)"
½"
17 (18, 19, 20)"

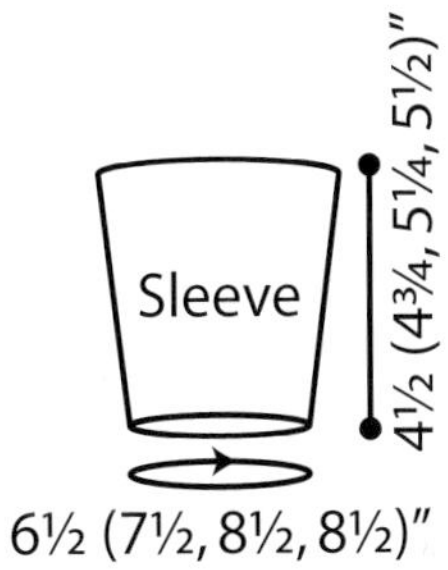
Sleeve
4½ (4¾, 5¼, 5½)"
6½ (7½, 8½, 8½)"

Note: Sleeves are worked directly into armholes after shoulders are seamed.

Rnd 8: With RS facing, join A with sc in any st, sc in each st around, join with sl st in beg sc. Fasten off.

Rnds 9–10: Repeat Rnds 6 and 7.

Rnd 11: With RS facing, join A with sc in any st, sc in each st around, join with sl st in beg sc.

Rnds 12–21 (23, 25, 27): Ch 1, turn, sc in each st around, join with sl st in beg sc.

Front

Row 1: Ch 1, turn, sc in first 32 (34, 36, 38) sts, leaving rem sts unworked—32 (34, 36, 38) sc.

Rows 2–3 (6, 8, 10): Ch 1, turn, sc in each st across.

Row 4 (7, 9, 11): Ch 1, turn, 2 sc in first st, sc in each st to last st, 2 sc in last st—34 (36, 38, 40) sc.

First Shoulder

Row 1: Ch 1, turn, 2 sc in first st, sc in next 8 (9, 10, 11) sts, leaving rem sts unworked—10 (11, 12, 13) sc.

Row 2: Ch 1, turn, sc in each st across.

Row 3: Ch 1, turn, sc in each st up to last 2 sts, sc2tog—9 (10, 11, 12) sc.

Rows 4–9: Repeat Rows 2–3 three times—6 (7, 8, 9) sc.

9 and 12 Months Only

Repeat Row 2 two more times.

All Sizes

Fasten off.

Second Shoulder

Row 1: Sk next 16 sts on last row of front, join A with sc in next st, sc in next 7 (8, 9, 10) sts, 2 sc in next st—10 (11, 12, 13) sc.

Row 2: Ch 1, turn, sc in each st across.

Row 3: Ch 1, turn, sc2tog, sc in each st across—9 (10, 11, 12) sc.

Rows 4–9: Repeat Rows 2–3 three times—6 (7, 8, 9) sc.

9 and 12 Months Only

Repeat Row 2 two more times.

All Sizes

Fasten off.

Back

Row 1: With WS facing, sk next 2 sts on last row of body, join A with sc in next st, sc in next 31 (33, 35, 37) sts—32 (34, 36, 38) sts.

Rows 2–13 (16, 20, 22): Ch 1, turn, sc in each st across. Fasten off. Sew shoulder seams together.

Bottom Band

Rnd 1: With RS facing, working in bottom loops of Rnd 1 of body, join B with sc in any st, sc in each st around, join with sl st in beg sc.

Rnds 2–3: Ch 1, do not turn, sc in each st around, join with sl st in beg sc.

Fasten off.

Neck Edging

Rnd 1: With RS facing, join B with sc in first skipped st on front of neck, sc in each st across; working in row ends of shoulder, sc in each row; sc in each st across back of neck; sc in end of each row of opposite shoulder; join with sl st in beg sc.

Rnds 2–3: Ch 1, do not turn, sc in each st around, join with sl st in beg sc.

Fasten off.

Sleeves (work 2)

Rnd 1 (RS): With RS facing, join A with sc in first skipped st at underarm, sc in next st; working in row ends, sc in each row around; join with sl st in beg sc—28 (34, 42, 46) sc.

Next 1 (2, 4, 6) Rnd(s): Ch 1, turn, sc2tog, sc in each st up to last 2 sts, sc2tog, join with sl st in beg sc—26 (30, 34, 34) sc.

Rnds 3–10 (4–11, 6–13, 8–15): Ch 1, turn, sc in each st around, join with sl st in beg sc.

Fasten off.

Rnd 11 (12, 14, 16): With RS facing, join B with sc in any st, sc in each st around, join with sl st in beg sc.

Rnd 12 (13, 15, 17): Ch 1, do not turn, sc in each st around, join with sl st in beg sc. Fasten off.

Rnd 13 (14, 16, 18): With RS facing, join A with sc in any st, sc in each st around, join with sl st in beg sc. Fasten off.

Rnds 14–15 (15–16, 17–18, 19–20): Repeat Rnds 11–12 (12–13, 14–15, 16–17).

Rnd 16 (17, 19, 21): With RS facing, join A with sc in any st, sc in each st around, join with sl st in beg sc.

Rnds 17–21 (18–22, 20–24, 22–26): Ch 1, turn, sc in each st around, join with sl st in beg sc.

Fasten off.

Rnds 22–23 (23–24, 25–26, 27–28): Repeat Rnds 11–12 (12–13, 14–15, 16–17).

Repeat for second sleeve.

Finishing

Weave in ends.

BOOTIES (make 2)

With C, ch 4.

Rnd 1 (RS): 9 dc in 4th ch from hook (first 3 ch count as first dc), join with sl st in top of beg ch-4—10 dc.

Rnd 2: Ch 1, turn, 2 sc in first st, sc in next 4 sts, 2 sc in next st, place marker in st just made, sc in each st around, join with sl st in beg sc—12 sc.

Move marker up on every round, placing it in the first sc of the 2-sc group as each rnd is worked.

Rnds 3–4: Ch 1, turn, 2 sc in first st, sc in each st up to marker, 2 sc in marked st, sc in each st around, join with sl st in beg sc—16 sc.

Fasten off.

Rnd 5: With RS facing, join D with sc in same st as joining, sc again in same st, sc in each st up to marker, 2 sc in marked st, sc in each st around, join with sl st in beg sc—18 sc.

Rnd 6: Ch 1, do not turn, 2 sc in first st, sc in each st up to marker, 2 sc in marked st, sc in each st around, join with sl st in beg sc—20 sc. Fasten off.

Rnd 7: With RS facing, join C with sc in same st as joining, sc again in same st, sc in each st up to marked st, 2 sc in marked st, sc in each st around, join with sl st in beg sc—22 sc.

Rnds 8–17: Ch 1, turn, sc in each st around, join with sl st in beg sc.

Heel

Take care to keep marker in same location.

Foot Opening Row: Ch 1, turn, sc in first 11 sts, leaving remaining sts unworked—11 sc.

Rnd 1: Ch 1, turn, sc in each st across, ch 11, join with sl st in beg sc—11 sc and 11 ch.

Rnd 2: Ch 1, turn, sc in each ch and st around, join with sl st in beg sc—22 sc.

From this point on, move marker to sc2tog as each rnd is worked.

Rnd 3: Ch 1, turn, sc2tog, sc in each st up to marker, sc2tog, sc in each st around, join with sl st in beg sc—20 sc. Fasten off.

Rnd 4: With RS facing, join D with sc in same st as joining, sc2tog, sc in each st up to marker, sc2tog, sc in each st around, join with sl st in beg sc—18 sc.

Rnd 5: Ch 1, do not turn, sc2tog, sc in each st up to marker, sc2tog, sc in each st around, join with sl st in beg sc—16 sc. Fasten off.

Rnd 6: With RS facing, join C with sc in same st as joining, sc2tog, sc in each st up to marker, sc2tog, sc in each st around, join with sl st in beg sc—14 sc.

Rnd 7: Ch 1, turn, sc2tog, sc in each st up to marker, sc2tog, sc in each st around, join with sl st in beg sc—12 sc.

Rnd 8: Ch 1, turn, [sc2tog] 6 times—6 sc. Fasten off. Sew remaining gap in heel closed.

Ankle

Rnd 1: With RS facing, join B with sc in first skipped st of Rnd 17; sc in each st across, sc over post of st of row end on foot opening, sc in bottom loop of each ch, sc in row end on opposite side, join with sl st in beg sc—24 sc.

Rnd 2: Ch 1, *sc2tog, sc in next 4 sts; repeat from * around, join with sl st in beg sc—20 sc.

Rnds 3–5: Ch 1, sc in each st around, join with sl st in beg sc.

Fasten off.

Finishing

Weave in ends.

HAT

With C, ch 4.

Rnd 1 (RS): 9 dc in 4th ch from hook (first 3 ch count as first dc), join with sl st in top of beg ch-4—10 dc.

Rnd 2: Ch 1, turn, 2 sc in first st, sc in next 4 sts, 2 sc in next st, place marker in st just made, sc in each st around, join with sl st in beg sc—12 sc.

Move marker up on every round, placing it in the first sc of the 2-sc group as each rnd is worked.

Rnds 3–6: Ch 1, turn, 2 sc in first st, sc in each st up to marker, 2 sc in marked st, sc in each st around, join with sl st in beg sc—20 sc. Remove marker.

Rnd 7: Ch 1, turn, 2 sc in first st, sc in next 3 sts, [2 sc in next st, sc in next 3 sts] 4 times, join with sl st in beg sc—25 sc.

Rnd 8: Ch 1, turn, sc in each st around, join with sl st in beg sc.

Rnd 9: Ch 1, turn, 2 sc in first st, sc in next 4 sts, [2 sc in next st, sc in next 4 sts] 4 times, join with sl st in beg sc—30 sc.

Rnd 10: Ch 1, turn, sc in each st around, join with sl st in beg sc. Fasten off.

Rnd 11: With RS facing, join D with sc in same st as joining, sc in same st, sc in next 5 sts, [2 sc in next st, sc in next 5 sts] 4 times, join with sl st in beg sc—35 sc.

Rnd 12: Ch 1, turn, sc in each st around, join with sl st in beg sc.

Rnd 13: Ch 1, turn, 2 sc in first st, sc in next 6 sts, [2 sc in next st, sc in next 6 sts] 4 times, join with sl st in beg sc—40 sc.

Rnd 14: With WS facing, join C with sc in same st as joining, sc in each st around, join with sl st in beg sc.

Rnd 15: Ch 1, turn, sc in each st around, join with sl st in beg sc.

Rnd 16: Ch 1, turn, 2 sc in first st, sc in next 7 sts, [2 sc in next st, sc in next 7 sts] 4 times, join with sl st in beg sc—45 sc.

Rnd 17: Ch 1, turn, sc in each st around, join with sl st in beg sc.

Rnd 18: Ch 1, turn, 2 sc in first st, sc in next 8 sts, [2 sc in next st, sc in next 8 sts] 4 times, join with sl st in beg sc—50 sc.

Rnd 19: Ch 1, turn, sc in each st around, join with sl st in beg sc.

Rnd 20: Ch 1, turn, 2 sc in first st, sc in next 9 sts, [2 sc in next st, sc in next 9 sts] 4 times, join with sl st in beg sc—55 sc.

Rnd 21: Ch 1, turn, sc in each st around, join with sl st in beg sc.

Rnd 22: Ch 1, turn, 2 sc in first st, sc in next 10 sts, [2 sc in next st, sc in next 10 sts] 4 times, join with sl st in beg sc—60 sc.

Rnds 23–35: Ch 1, turn, sc in each st around, join with sl st in beg sc.

Fasten off.

Rnd 36: With RS facing, join B with sc in any st, sc in each st around, join with sl st in beg sc.

Rnd 37: Ch 1, turn, sc in each st around, join with sl st in beg sc. Fasten off.

Lacing

Center Strip

With D, ch 16.

Row 1: Dc in 4th ch from hook (first 3 ch count as first dc) and in each ch across—14 dc. Do not fasten off.

Cross Laces

Rnd 1: Ch 1, working over post of last st, 2 sc in end of center strip, ch 1, working in bottom loops of starting ch, *sl st in next 3 sts, ch 5, sc in 2nd ch from hook and in next 3 ch, sl st in same st as last sl st ** repeat from * to ** 3 more times, sl st in next 2 sts, ch 1, 2 sc over post of end of center strip, ch 1, repeat from * to ** 4 times, sl st in next 2 sts, ch 1, join with sl st in beg sc. Fasten off, leaving a long tail for sewing.

Finishing

Sew lacing to hat, using the photo as a guide for placement. Weave in ends.

Varsity Cheerleader Girl Dress and Headband

SKILL LEVEL

EASY

Your little girl will be all set to help cheer your team to victory when you dress her in this adorable dress, which features a full skirt with vertical stripes. The adorable headband is the perfect finishing touch.

83

YARN
Plymouth Yarn Cleo (100% Mercerized Pima Cotton;
   1.75 oz/50 g; 125 yd./114 m)
#0106 Lemon (A): 3 hanks
#0500 Black (B): 2 hanks

CROCHET HOOK
U.S. size F-5 (3.75 mm) or size needed to obtain
   gauge

ADDITIONAL MATERIALS
Stitch markers
Yarn needle
15 (16, 17, 18) in. [38 (41, 43, 46) cm] elastic, 1 in.
   (25 mm) wide

SIZES
3 (6, 9, 12) months
Note: Instructions are given for smallest size;
   changes for larger sizes are given in parentheses.

FINISHED MEASUREMENTS
Chest: 17 (18, 19, 20) in. [43 (45.5, 48.5, 51) cm]
Length: 10½ (11¼, 13, 13¾) in. [26.5 (28.5, 33,
   35) cm]

GAUGE
16 sc and 20 rows/rnds = 4 in. (10 cm)

GIRL

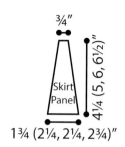

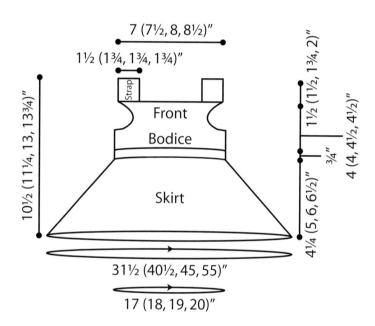

NOTES
Skirt panels are made first and sewn together.
Waistband is worked on top of skirt. Bodice is
worked on top of waistband. Front and back
are split and worked in rows up to shoulders.

DRESS
Skirt
Panels (make 18 (18, 20, 20): 9 (9, 10, 10)
with A and 9 (9, 10, 10) with B)
Ch 4.
Row 1: Sc in 2nd ch from hook and in each ch across—
   3 sc.
Rows 2–6: Ch 1, turn, sc in each st across.
Row 7: Ch 1, turn, 2 sc in first st, sc in each st up to last
   st, 2 sc in last st—5 sc.
Rows 8–12: Repeat Rows 2–6.

Rows 13–18 (24, 24, 30): Repeat last 6 rows 1 (2, 2, 3)
   times—7 (9, 9, 11) sc.
Next 3 (1, 5, 3) Row(s): Ch 1, turn, sc in each st across.
Fasten off.

Side Edging
Row 1 (RS): Working in ends of rows and using the
   opposite color from the one used in the panel, join
   yarn with sl st in last row of panel, sl st in each row,
   ch 1, sl st in center bottom loop of Row 1 of panel,
   ch 1, sl st in each row to end—43 (51, 61, 67) sl sts
   and 2 ch-1 sps. Fasten off.

Assembly

With yarn needle, whipstitch panels together through BLO of sl sts, alternating panel colors.

Bottom Band

Rnd 1: With RS facing, join B with sc in any st on last row of panels. Sc evenly spaced around lower edge of skirt; join with sl st in beg sc.

Rnds 2–3: Ch 1, sc in each st around, join with sl st in beg sc.

Fasten off.

Waistband

Rnd 1: With RS facing, working over sl sts and ch-1 sps, join B with sc in any st on Row 1 of any panel; work 67 (71, 75, 79) more sc evenly spaced around top edge of skirt; join with sl st in beg sc—68 (72, 76, 80) sc.

Rnds 2–4: Ch 1, sc in each st around, join with sl st in beg sc.

Fasten off.

Bodice

Rnd 1: With RS facing, join A with sc in any st, sc in each st around, join with sl st in beg sc.

Rnds 2–9 (9, 11, 11): Ch 1, turn, sc in each st around, join with sl st in beg sc.

Front

Row 1 (WS): Ch 1, turn, sc in first 32 (34, 36, 38) sts, leaving rem sts unworked—32 (34, 36, 38) sc.

Rows 2–7: Ch 1, turn, sc2tog, sc in each st up to last 2 sts, sc2tog—20 (22, 24, 26) sc.

Rows 8–11: Ch 1, turn, 2 sc in first st, sc in each st up to last st, 2 sc in last st—28 (30, 32, 34) sc.

First Strap

Row 1: Ch 1, turn, sc in first 7 (8, 9, 10) sts, leaving rem sts unworked—7 (8, 9, 10) sc.

Row 2: Ch 1, turn, sc in each st across.

Row 3: Ch 1, turn, sc in each st up to last 2 sts, sc2tog—6 (7, 8, 9) sc.

3 and 6 Months Only

Rows 4–7 (8): Ch 1, turn, sc in each st across—6 (7) sc.

Fasten off.

9 and 12 Months Only

Rows 4–5 (7): Repeat Rows 2 and 3 one (two) more times—7 (7) sc.

Rows 6–9 (8–10): Ch 1, turn, sc in each st across.

Fasten off.

Second Strap

Row 1: Sk next 14 sts on last row of front, join A with sc in next st, sc in next 6 (7, 8, 9) sts—7 (8, 9, 10) sc.

Row 2: Ch 1, turn, sc in each st across.

Row 3: Ch 1, turn, sc2tog, sc in each st across—6 (7, 8, 9) sc.

Rows 4–7 (8, 9, 10): Work same as Rows 4–7 (8, 9, 10) of first strap—6 (7, 7, 7) sc.

Fasten off.

Back

Row 1: With WS facing, sk next 2 sts on last row of bodice, join A with sc in next st, sc in next 31 (33, 35, 37) sts, leaving rem sts unworked—32 (34, 36, 38) sts.

Rows 2–11: Work same as Rows 2–11 of front.

First and Second Strap

Work same as front straps.
Sew shoulder seams together.

Neck Edging

Rnd 1: With RS facing, join B with sc in first skipped st between straps on front or back; sc in each st; working in row ends of first strap, sc in each row; sc in each skipped st on opposite side; sc in each row of second strap, join with sl st in beg sc—56 (60, 64, 68) sc.

Rnd 2: Ch 1, sc in each st around, join with sl st in beg sc. Fasten off.

Armhole Edging (work 2)

Rnd 1: With RS facing, join B with sc in first skipped st of either underarm, sc in next st; working in row ends, sc in each row, join with sl st in beg sc—38 (40, 42, 44) sc.

Rnd 2: Ch 1, (sc2tog) 3 times, sc in each st up to last 6 sts, (sc2tog) 3 times, join with sl st in beg sc—32 (34, 36, 38) sc.

Rnd 3: Ch 1, sc in each st around, join with sl st in beg sc. Fasten off.

Finishing

Weave in ends.

HEADBAND

With B, ch 7.

Row 1: Sc in 2nd ch from hook and each ch across—6 sc.

Row 2: Ch 1, turn, sc in each st across.

Repeat Row 2 until headband measures desired length. Fasten off, leaving a long tail for sewing. Folding piece in half, sew last row to bottom loops of row 1.

Cut elastic to 1 in. (2.5 cm) longer than desired length. Make a loop of the elastic, overlapping ½ in. (13 mm) of the ends; sew in place. Slide headband over elastic. Join A with sl st in any row, ch 1, *working through row ends and through both thicknesses of fabric, sl st in next row end, ch 1; repeat from * around. Fasten off.

Flower

With A, ch 5, join with sl st to form ring.

Rnd 1: Ch 1, 2 sc in each ch around, join with sl st in beg sc—10 sc.

Rnd 2: Ch 1, working in FLO, sc in each st around, join with sl st in beg sc.

Rnd 3: Ch 7, sl st in same st as joining, ch 7, *(sl st, ch 7, sl st) in next st, ch 7; repeat from * around. Fasten off, leaving a long tail for sewing.

Finishing

Sew flower to headband. Weave in ends.

October

Boo!

It's Halloween, and time to dress baby up in his or her first costume. What better choice than this adorable dinosaur outfit? The main stitch in the costume is single crochet (represented on an easy-to-follow chart), which means you'll be able to complete this costume in no time flat. Don't worry about the tail: It's very flexible and shifts out of the way so baby will still be able to sit down comfortably.

Stanley or Stella the Stegosaurus Costume

SKILL LEVEL

EASY

Your little boy or girl will look quite ferocious dressed in this dinosaur costume covered with spines. (Although some kids will prefer to portray the gentle vegetarian side of this dinosaur's personality!) Make it in blue, pink, or any other color combination.

YARN

Red Heart With Love (100% Acrylic;
7 oz/198 g; 370 yd./338 m)

Blue version

#1502 Iced Aqua (A): 1 skein

#1803 Blue Hawaii (B): 1 skein

Pink version

#1704 Bubble Gum (A): 1 skein

#1703 Candy Pink (B): 1 skein

CROCHET HOOK

U.S. size I-9 (5.5 mm) or size needed
to obtain gauge

ADDITIONAL MATERIALS

Yarn needle

Stitch markers

Fiberfill

Straight pins

3 size 4 snaps

SIZES

0–3 months (3–6 months, 6–9 months,
9–12 months)

Note: Instructions are given for smallest
size; changes for larger sizes are given
in parentheses.

FINISHED MEASUREMENTS

Chest: 17¼ (18¾, 19¼, 20) in. [44 (47.5,
49, 51) cm]

Length: 17 (18½, 20, 21) in. [43 (47, 51,
53.5) cm]

Hat Circumference: 16¾ in. (42.5cm)

GAUGE

12 sc and 14 rows/rounds = 4 in. (10 cm)

SPECIAL STITCH

Spike: Working over post of st, (sc, hdc, dc, tr, ch 2, sc
in 2nd ch from hook [picot made], sl st in top of tr, dc,
hdc, sc) in same sp.

NOTES

1. To change color, work last stitch of old color to last
   yarn over. Yarn over with new color and draw through
   all loops on hook to complete stitch. Proceed with

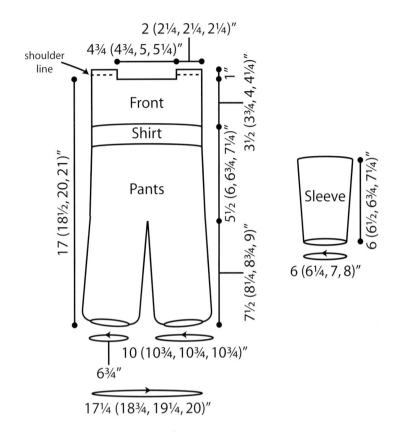

Notes: Total length includes only half height of
shoulders. Sleeves are worked directly into
armholes after shoulders are seamed

new color. Carry colors not in use up back of piece
until needed again.

2. The tummy circle is worked over the center 22 (24,
   25, 26) sts of front. Markers are used to indicate
   where to begin and end the tummy circle. The
   tummy circle is worked by reading the chart for the
   desired size. Read RS rows of the chart from right to
   left and WS rows from left to right.

3. The pants are made first, from the waist down. Half
   of the tummy circle is worked when the pants are
   made. The other half of the tummy circle is worked
   when the shirt is made.

4. The shirt is added to the top of the waist, working in
   rounds, then split for the front and two back panels.

Tummy Circle Chart - Size 9-12 months

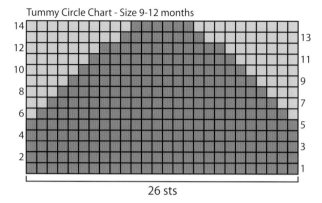

26 sts

Tummy Circle Chart - Size 6-9 months

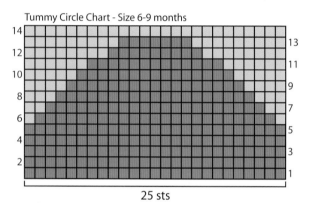

25 sts

Tummy Circle Chart - Size 3-6 months

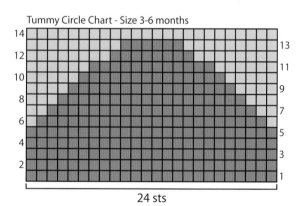

24 sts

Tummy Circle Chart - Size 0-3 months

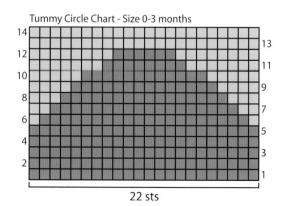

22 sts

COSTUME
Pants
With A, ch 52 (56, 58, 60), join with sl st to form ring.

Rnd 1 (RS): Ch 1, sc in first 2 ch, changing to B in second st; sc in next 22 (24, 25, 26) ch (this is row 1 of chart), changing to A in last st; sc in each remaining ch around, join with sl st in beg sc—52 (56, 58, 60) sc.

Place markers on the 3rd st and the 24th (26th, 27th, 28th) sts. The markers indicate where to begin and end the tummy circle chart. The first stitch of the chart should be worked in the first marked st and the last st of the chart should be worked in the last marked st. Move the markers up as each rnd is worked. Place two more markers in the bottom loops of Rnd 1 directly below the first two markers. These markers will be used later when the shirt is worked. Do not move these markers until working the shirt.

Rnds 2–14: Ch 1, turn, sc in each st to first marker, work next row of chart over next 22 (24, 25, 26) sts (last st of chart is worked in 2nd marked st), sc in each remaining st around, join with sl st in beg sc.

Fasten off B. Continue with A only. Remove markers for pants. Do not remove markers for shirt.

Next 0 (2, 4, 6) Rnds: Ch 1, sc in each st around, join with sl st in beg sc.

Fasten off.

Gusset
Row 1: With RS facing, sk first 12 (13, 13, 13) sts, join A with sc in next st, sc in next 1 (2, 2, 3) sts—2 (3, 3, 4) sts.

Rows 2–6: Ch 1, turn, sc in each st across.

Fasten off. Sew sts of last row to corresponding 2 (3, 3, 4) sts on back, leaving 24 (26, 26, 26) sts open on each side for legs.

Legs (work 2)
Rnd 1: Working over row ends of gusset, with RS facing, join A with sc in 4th row, sc in next 2 rows, sc in each st around leg opening, sc in last 3 rows of gusset, join with sl st in beg sc—30 (32, 32, 32) sc.

Rnds 2–24 (26, 28, 29): Ch 1, turn, sc in each st around, join with sl st in beg sc.

Fasten off. Repeat for second leg.

Cuff (work 2)

Rnd 1: With RS facing, join B with sc in any st at bottom of leg, sc in next 3 (1, 1, 1) sts, sc2tog, *sc in next 2 sts, sc2tog; repeat from * around, join with sl st in beg sc—23 (24, 24, 24) sc.

Rnd 2: Ch 1, sc in each st around, join with sl st in beg sc.

Rnd 3: Ch 1, sc in first 1 (0, 0, 0) sts, *sc in next 5 (4, 4, 4) sts, sc2tog; repeat from * around, join with sl st in beg sc—20 sc.

Fasten off. Repeat for second leg.

Shirt

Rnd 1 (RS): With RS facing, working in bottom loops of Rnd 1 of pants, sk first 2 sts following tummy circle, join A with sc in next st, sc in each st to first marker, work row 1 of chart over next 22 (24, 25, 26) sts (the first and last st of chart should be worked in the marked sts), sc in each st around, join with sl st in beg sc.

Rnds 2–5: Repeat Rnds 2–5 of pants.

Front

Row 1 (WS): Ch 1, turn, sc in each st to first marker, work Row 6 of chart to next marker, sc in next 2 sts, leaving rem sts unworked—26 (28, 29, 30) sc.

Rows 2–9: Ch 1, turn, sc in each st to first marker, work next row of chart to next marker, sc in each st across. Fasten off B. Continue with A only. Remove markers.

Rows 10–12 (13, 14, 15): Ch 1, turn, sc in each st across.

FIRST SHOULDER

Row 1: Ch 1, turn, sc in first 6 (7, 7, 7) sts, leaving rem sts unworked—6 (7, 7, 7) sc.

Rows 2–3: Ch 1, turn, sc in each st across. Fasten off.

SECOND SHOULDER

Row 1: Sk next 14 (14, 15, 16) unworked sts following first shoulder and join A with sc in next st, sc in next 5 (6, 6, 6) sts.

Rows 2–3: Ch 1, turn, sc in each st across. Fasten off.

First Back Panel

Row 1: With RS facing, join A with sc in first unworked st following front, sc in next 10 (11, 11, 12) sts—11 (12, 12, 13) sc.

Rows 2–12 (13, 14, 15): Ch 1, turn, sc in each st across. Fasten off.

Second Back Panel

Row 1: With RS facing, sk next 4 (4, 5, 4) sts following first back panel, join A with sc in next st, sc in next 10 (11, 11, 12) sts—11 (12, 12, 13) sc.

Rows 2–12 (13, 14, 15): Ch 1, turn, sc in each st across. Fasten off.

Sew shoulder seams together.

Snap Band

LEFT BAND

Row 1: With RS facing, join A with sl st in last skipped st between back panels and, working over row ends of left back panel, sc in each row of left back panel—12 (13, 14, 15) sc and 1 sl st.

Row 2: Ch 1, turn, sc in each st, sl st in same st as previous sl st.

Row 3: Turn, sc in each st across.

Row 4: Ch 1, turn, sc in each st, sl st in next skipped st between back panels.

Row 5: Turn, sc in each st across.

6–9 and 9–12 Months Only

Rows 6–7: Repeat Rows 4–5.

All Sizes

Fasten off. Sew 3 snap backs evenly spaced and centered over last 3 rows of band.

RIGHT BAND

Row 1: With WS facing, working over row ends of right back panel, join A with sl st in first skipped st between back panels, sc in each row of right back panel—12 (13, 14, 15) sc and 1 sl st.

Rows 2–5 (5, 7, 7): Work same as Rows 2–5 (5, 7, 7) of left band.

Fasten off. Sew 3 snap fronts evenly spaced and centered over last 3 rows of band, opposite snap backs on other band.

Neck Edging

Row 1: Working over row ends, join A with sc in last row of left snap band, sc in each row, sc in each row of left shoulder, sc in each st across last row of front, sc in each row of right shoulder, sc in each row of right snap band. Fasten off.

Sleeves (work 2)

Rnd 1: With RS facing, working over row ends around armhole opening, join A with sc in any row, sc in each row around, join with sl st in beg sc—27 (29, 31, 33) sc.

Rnd 2: Ch 1, turn, sc in first 7 (6, 8, 9) sts, sc2tog, *sc in next 7 (5, 5, 9) sts, sc2tog; repeat from * around, join with sl st in beg sc—24 (25, 27, 30) sc.

Rnd 3: Ch 1, turn, sc in each st around, join with sl st in beg sc.

Rnd 4: Ch 1, turn, sc in first 6 (5, 7, 8) sts, sc2tog, *sc in next 6 (4, 4, 8) sts, sc2tog; repeat from * around, join with sl st in beg sc—21 (21, 23, 27) sc.

Rnd 5: Ch 1, turn, sc in each st around, join with sl st in beg sc.

Rnd 6: Ch 1, turn, sc in first 5 (5, 7, 7) sts, sc2tog, *sc in next 5 (5, 5, 7) sts, sc2tog; repeat from * around, join with sl st in beg sc—18 (19, 21, 24) sc.

Rnds 7–20 (22, 23, 24): Ch 1, turn, sc in each st around, join with sl st in beg sc.

Fasten off.

Edging Rnd: Join B with sc in any st, sc in each st around, join with sl st in beg sc. Fasten off.

Repeat for second sleeve.

Tail

With A, ch 27, join with sl st to form ring.

Rnd 1: Ch 1, sc in each ch around; do not join, but work in continuous rnds (spiral)—27 sc.

Place marker to indicate beginning of rnd. Move marker up as each rnd is completed.

Rnds 2–27: Ch 1, sc2tog, sc in each st around—1 sc.

Fasten off. Lightly stuff tail with fiberfill and shape. Centering tail over seat of pants, pin to hold, then sew in place.

Tail Spikes

With B, loosely ch 41.

Row 1: Sc in 2nd ch from hook and each ch across— 40 sc.

Row 2: Ch 1, turn, working over post of sts, spike in first st, *skip next 2 sts, spike in next st; repeat from * across.

Fasten off, leaving a long tail for sewing. Pin strip in place from tip of tail to top of right snap band. Working on back side of strip, sew in place.

Finishing

Weave in ends.

HAT

With A, ch 3, join with sl st to form ring.

Rnd 1 (RS): Ch 1, 10 sc in ring, mark last st—10 sc.

Rnd 2: 2 sc in each st around—20 sc.

Rnd 3: Sc in each st around.

Rnd 4: *Sc in next st, 2 sc in next st; repeat from * around—30 sc.

Rnd 5: Sc in each st around.

Rnd 6: *Sc in next 2 sts, 2 sc in next st; repeat from * around—40 sc.

Rnd 7: Sc in each st around.

Rnd 8: *Sc in next 3 sts, 2 sc in next st; repeat from * around—50 sc.

Rnds 9–20: Sc in each st around.

After last rnd, sl st in next st. Fasten off.

Hat Spikes

With B, loosely ch 32.

Row 1: Sc in 2nd ch from hook and each ch across— 31 sc.

Row 2: Ch 1, turn, working over post of sts, spike in first st, *skip next 2 sts, spike in next st; repeat from * across.

Fasten off, leaving a long tail for sewing. Pin strip in place using photos for guide to placement. Working on back side of strip, sew in place.

Finishing

Weave in ends.

CHAPTER ELEVEN

November

Giving Thanks

I chose yarns in fall colors reminiscent of autumn leaves and Thanksgiving for this month's outfits. Baby will be toasty warm in the crisp autumn air when wearing the cozy sweater, hat, and booties. The color combinations of either sweater can be worn just as easily by a boy or a girl, so make your baby's sweater in whichever colors you prefer—or create your own combination.

95

Fall Festival Cardigan, Hat, and Booties

Your little boy or girl will be as cozy as can be in this beautiful striped sweater with contrasting sleeves. The leaf-shaped buttons add a festive touch to the outfit.

96

YARN

Valley Yarns Colrain (50% Merino, 50% Tencel; 1.76 oz/50 g; 109 yd./100 m)

Approximately 150 yd. (137 m) color A (main color) plus 300 yd. (274 m) total in assorted contrasting colors.

Black

Burgundy

Caramel

Chestnut

Grey Olive

Jungle Green

Natural

Navajo Red

Samples pictured use Burgundy for color A in the boy sweater and Natural for color A in the girl sweater.

CROCHET HOOK

U.S. size H-8 (5 mm) or size needed to obtain gauge

ADDITIONAL MATERIALS

Blumenthal Lansing Favorite Findings #550000535, Falling Leaves Buttons

Yarn needle

SIZES

3 (6, 9, 12) months

Note: Instructions are given for smallest size; changes for larger sizes are given in parentheses.

FINISHED MEASUREMENTS

Cardigan Chest: 17¾ (18½, 19, 19¾) in. [45 (47, 48.5, 50) cm], including front bands, buttoned

Cardigan Length: 7½ (8, 8½, 9) in. [19 (20.5, 21.5, 23) cm]

Hat Circumference: 15½ in. (39.5 cm)

Bootie Circumference: 6 in. (15 cm)

Bootie Length: 5 in. (12.5 cm)

GAUGE

12 sc and 16 rows = 4 in. (10 cm)

NOTES

1. Sweater is worked in one piece from lower edge to underarm. The piece is then divided for armholes and back and fronts worked separately to shoulders.
2. Sleeves are worked directly into armhole openings.
3. Color is changed at the end of every other row throughout body of cardigan. Work in any stripe sequence desired. Write down the stripe sequence you use so that you can use the same sequence for back and both fronts. Sleeves are worked in main color (A), with striped cuffs. Select any color as the main color (A).
4. To change color, work last stitch of old color to last yarn over. Yarn over with new color and draw through all loops on hook to complete stitch. Fasten off old color. Proceed with new color.

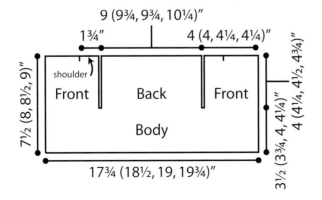

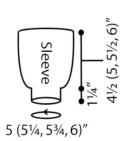

Note: Sleeves are worked directly into armholes after shoulders are seamed

SWEATER
Body

With any color, ch 54 (56, 58, 60).

Row 1 (RS): Sc in 2nd ch from hook and in each ch across—53 (55, 57, 59) sc.

Row 2: Ch 1, turn, sc in each st across, changing to next color in last st.

Row 3: Ch 1, turn, sc in each st across.

Repeat last row and continue to change color at the end of every other row in stripe sequence of your choice until a total of 14 (15, 16, 17) rows have been worked.

First Front

Continue to change color at the end of every other row throughout body.

Row 1: Ch 1, turn, sc in first 12 (12, 13, 13) sts, leaving remaining sts unworked—12 (12, 13, 13) sc.

Rows 2–16 (17, 18, 19): Ch 1, turn, sc in each st across.

Fasten off.

Back

Row 1: Sk next unworked st following first front (for underarm); working in same stripe sequence as first front, join yarn with sc in next st, sc in next 26 (28, 28, 30) sts, leaving remaining sts unworked—27 (29, 29, 31) sc.

Rows 2–16 (17, 18, 19): Ch 1, turn, sc in each st across. Continue to change color at the end of every other row, following same stripe sequence as in first front.

Fasten off.

Second Front

Row 1: Sk next unworked st following back; working in same stripe sequence as first front and back, join yarn with sc in next st, sc in next 11 (11, 12, 12) sts, leaving remaining sts unworked—12 (12, 13, 13) sc.

Rows 2–16 (17, 18, 19): Ch 1, turn, sc in each st across. Continue to change color at the end of every other row, following same stripe sequence as in first front and back.

Fasten off.

Assembly

Matching up sts of last row on first front with sts of last row on back, sew together 6 sts at outside edge for shoulder. Repeat for second front.

Right Front Band

Row 1: Working over posts of sts at row ends, join A with sl st in first row of right front, ch 1, sc2tog over first 2 rows, [ch 1, sc2tog over next 2 rows] 14 (15, 16, 17) times—15 (16, 17, 18) sc and 14 (15, 16, 17) ch-1 sps.

Rows 2–5: Ch 1, turn, sc in first st, *ch 1, sc in next st; repeat from * across.

Fasten off.

Left Front Band

Row 1: Working over posts of sts at row ends, join A with sl st in last row of left front, ch 1, sc2tog over first 2 rows, [ch 1, sc2tog over next 2 rows] 14 (15, 16, 17) times—15 (16, 17, 18) sc and 14 (15, 16, 17) ch-1 sps.

Rows 2–5: Ch 1, turn, sc in first st, *ch 1, sc in next st; repeat from * across.

Fasten off.

Collar

Row 1: With RS facing, join A with sc in first st on last row of right front band, sc again in same st; working in sts across last row of right front band, across last row of back, and in sts across last row of left front band; *sc in next st, 2 sc in next st; repeat from * to end—41 (44, 47, 50) sc.

Rows 2–8: Ch 1, turn, sc in each st across.

Fasten off.

Sleeves (work 2)

Rnd 1: With RS facing, join A with sc in skipped st at underarm on either side, working over posts of sts at row ends around armhole, ch 1, *sc2tog, ch 1; repeat from * around, join with sl st in beg sc—17 (18, 19, 20) sc and 17 (18, 19, 20) ch-1 sps.

Rnds 2–3: Ch 1, turn, sc2tog (working over first ch-1 sp and next sc), ch 1, *sc in next st, ch 1; repeat from * around, skipping the last sc, join with sl st in beg sc—15 (16, 17, 18) sc and 15 (16, 17, 18) ch-1 sps.

Rnds 4–18 (20, 22, 24): Ch 1, turn, sc in first st, ch 1, *sc in next st, ch 1; repeat from * around, join with sl st in beg sc.

Fasten off.

Cuffs (work 2)

Rnd 1: With RS facing, join any color with sc in any st at end of sleeve, sc in each st around (skipping the ch-1 sps), join with sl st in beg sc—15 (16, 17, 18) sc.

Rnd 2: Ch 1, sc in each st around, changing to next color in last st, join with sl st in beg sc.

Continue to change color at the end of every other round in stripe sequence of your choice.

Rnds 3–5: Ch 1, sc in each st around, join with sl st in beg sc.

Repeat for second sleeve.

Finishing

Weave in ends. Evenly spacing 5 buttons on button band, sew buttons to right front for boy and left front for girl. Button into ch-1 spaces on opposite band.

HAT

With any color, ch 2.

Rnd 1: Work 10 sc in 2nd ch from hook, join with sl st in beg sc—10 sc.

Rnd 2: Ch 1, sc in each st around, changing to next color in last st; join with sl st in beg sc.

Continue to change color at the end of every other rnd in stripe sequence of your choice.

Rnd 3: Ch 1, 2 sc in each st around, join with sl st in beg sc—20 sc.

Rnd 4: Ch 1, 2 sc in first st, sc in next st, *2 sc in next st, sc in next st; repeat from * around, join with sl st in beg sc—30 sc.

Rnd 5: Ch 1, sc in each st around, join with sl st in beg sc.

Rnd 6: Ch 1, 2 sc in first st, sc in next 2 sts, *2 sc in next st, sc in next 2 sts; repeat from * around, join with sl st in beg sc—40 sc.

Rnd 7: Ch 1, sc in each st around, join with sl st in beg sc.

Rnd 8: Ch 1, 2 sc in first st, sc in next 3 sts, *2 sc in next st, sc in next 3 sts; repeat from * around, join with sl st in beg sc—50 sc.

Rnd 9: Ch 1, 2 sc in first st, sc in next 4 sts, *2 sc in next st, sc in next 4 sts; repeat from * around, join with sl st in beg sc—60 sc.

Rnd 10: Ch 1, sc in each st around, join with sl st in beg sc.

Rnd 11: Ch 1, sc2tog, sc in next 4 sts, *sc2tog, sc in next 4 sts; repeat from * around, join with sl st in beg sc—50 sc.

Rnds 12–30: Ch 1, sc in each st around, join with sl st in beg sc.

Fasten off.

Finishing

Weave in ends. Roll up last 5 rnds to form brim.

BOOTIES (make 2)

With any color, ch 2.

Rnd 1: 10 sc in 2nd ch from hook, join with sl st in beg sc—10 sc.

Rnd 2: Ch 1, turn, sc in each st around, changing to next color in last st; join with sl st in beg sc.

Continue to change color at the end of every other rnd in stripe sequence of your choice.

Rnd 3: Ch 1, turn, 2 sc in each st around, join with sl st in beg sc—20 sc.

Rnds 4–16: Ch 1, turn, sc in each st around, join with sl st in beg sc.

Do not fasten off.

Ankle

Rnd 1: Ch 1, turn, sc in first 12 sts, leaving remaining 8 sts unworked, ch 8, join with sl st in beg sc—12 sc and 1 ch-8 sp.

Rnd 2: Ch 1, turn, sc in each ch and st around, join with sl st in beg sc—20 sc.

Rnds 3–6: Ch 1, turn, sc in each st around, join with sl st in beg sc.

Fasten off.

Heel

Row 1: With RS facing, join any yarn with sc in first skipped st on rnd 1 of ankle, sc in next 2 sts, 2 sc in next 2 sts, sc in next 3 sts, sc over post of st on Rnd 1 of ankle; working in bottom loops of ch, sc in next 8 ch; sc over post of st at opposite end of Rnd 1 on ankle, join with sl st in beg sc—20 sc.

Rnds 2–4: Ch 1, turn, sc in each st around, join with sl st in beg sc.

Rnds 5–6: Ch 1, turn, (sc2tog) around, join with sl st in beg sc—5 sc.

Fasten off, leaving a long tail for sewing. Sew opening closed.

CHAPTER TWELVE

December

Happy Holidays

Baby's first holiday season is a once-in-a-lifetime occasion. Every parent will want a special outfit for December's many photo opportunities. Whether it's baby's first visit with Santa, taking a picture for the family holiday card, attending a party, or opening presents, these festive, sparkly outfits will make baby's first holiday season exceptional and memorable.

Santa's Little Helper Boy Pants and Bow Tie

SKILL LEVEL

EASY

Dress your handsome little guy in this festive outfit, and he'll be all set to help Santa check the names on the Nice List. He'll look just like a miniature Santa himself in these red pants with black trim and suspenders.

Add the red bow tie and your little boy will light up the party.

YARN
Lion Brand Vanna's Glamour (96% Acrylic, 4% Metallic
   Polyester; 1.75 oz/50 g; 202 yd./185 m)
#114 Red Stone (A): 2 balls
#153 Onyx (B): 1 ball

CROCHET HOOK
U.S. size F-5 (3.75 mm) or size needed to obtain gauge

ADDITIONAL MATERIALS
Yarn needle
2 shank buttons, ¾ in. (19 mm) in diameter
Sewing needle and matching thread
One size 4 sew-on snap

SIZES
3 (6, 9, 12) months
Note: Instructions are given for smallest size; changes for
   larger sizes are given in parentheses.

FINISHED MEASUREMENTS
Waist: 15½ (16½, 17, 17¼) in. [39.5 (42, 43, 44) cm]
Length: 13 (14¼, 15½, 16¾) in. [33 (36, 39.5, 42.5) cm],
   not including suspenders

GAUGE
18 sc and 20 rows = 4 in. (10 cm)

PANTS
With A, ch 70 (74, 76, 78), join with sl st to form ring.
Rnd 1: Sc in 2nd ch from hook and each ch around, join
   with sl st in beg sc—70 (74, 76, 78) sc.
Rnds 2–23 (25, 27, 29): Ch 1, turn, sc in each st around,
   join with sl st in beg sc.

Gusset
Row 1: Ch 1, turn, sc in first 8 (10, 10, 10) sts, leaving
   rem sts unworked—8 (10, 10, 10) sc.
Rows 2–6 (7, 7, 7): Ch 1, turn, sc in each st across. Place
   marker in last st made (it will be used later for posi-
   tioning the suspenders).
Fasten off, leaving a long tail for sewing.
Sk next 27 (27, 28, 29) sts on last rnd of pants and sew
   last row of gusset to next 8 (10, 10, 10) sts.

BOY

Suspenders

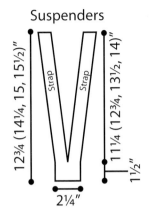

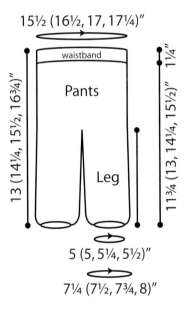

Leg
Rnd 1: Working over row ends on one side of gusset,
   join A with sc in 4th row of gusset, sc in next 2 (3, 3,
   3) rows, sc in each st on last rnd of pants around leg
   opening, sc in last 3 rows of gusset, join with sl st in
   beg sc—33 (34, 35, 36) sc.
Rnds 2–30 (34, 38, 42): Ch 1, turn, sc in each st around,
   join with sl st in beg sc.
Fasten off.

Cuff

Rnd 1: Join B with sc in any st of end of leg; sc in each st around, join with sl st in beg sc.

Rnd 2: Ch 1, sc2tog, sc in next 1 (2, 3, 4) sts, *sc2tog, sc in next 4 sts; repeat from * around, join with sl st in beg sc—27 (28, 29, 30) sc.

Rnd 3: Ch 1, sc in each st around, join with sl st in beg sc.

Rnd 4: Repeat Rnd 2—22 (23, 24, 25) sc.

Rnds 5–6: Ch 1, sc in each st around, join with sl st in beg sc.

Fasten off.

Waistband

Rnd 1: Laying pants flat to center gusset with 35 (37, 38, 39) sts on front and 35 (37, 38, 39) sts on back, working in bottom loops of Rnd 1, join B with sc in first st at beginning of front, sc in each st around, join with sl st in beg sc—70 (74, 76, 78) sc.

Rnds 2–3: Ch 1, sc in each st around, join with sl st in beg sc.

Rnd 4: Ch 1, sc in first 9 (10, 10, 10) sts, ch 2, sk next 2 sts (for first buttonhole), sc in next 13 (13, 14, 15) sts, ch 2, sk next 2 sts (for 2nd buttonhole), sc in each st around, join with sl st in beg sc—66 (70, 72, 74) sc and 2 ch-2 sps.

Rnd 5: Ch 1, sc in each st and ch around, join with sl st in beg sc—70 (74, 76, 78) sc.

Rnd 6: Ch 1, sc in each st around, join with sl st in beg sc.

Fasten off.

Suspenders

Row 1: For 3 month size, join B with sc in the st directly above the st that is 1 st before the first (marked) gusset st. For all other sizes, join B with sc in the st directly above the first (marked) gusset st, sc in next 9 sts—10 sc. Remove gusset marker.

Rows 2–7: Ch 1, turn, sc in each st across.

First Strap

Row 1: Ch 1, turn, sc in first 5 sts, leaving remaining sts unworked—5 sc.

Rows 2–56 (64, 68, 70): Ch 1, turn, sc in each st across. Fasten off.

Second Strap

Row 1: Join B with sc in next unworked st after first strap, sc in next 4 sts.

Rows 2–56 (64, 68, 70): Ch 1, turn, sc in each st across. Fasten off.

Edging

Row 1: Working in row ends, join B with sl st in Row 1 of suspenders, sl st in each row around each side of each strap and the back of the suspenders.

Finishing

Using sewing needle and matching thread, sew a button to the end of each strap. Weave in ends.

BOW TIE

Bow Half (make 2)

With A, ch 4.

Row 1: Sc in 2nd ch from hook and each ch across—3 sc.

Row 2: Ch 1, turn, sc in each st across.

Row 3: Ch 1, turn, 2 sc in first st, sc in each st to last st, 2 sc in last st—5 sc.

Rows 4–9: Repeat last 2 rows 3 times—11 sc.

Rows 10–13: Ch 1, turn, sc in each st across.

Row 14: Ch 1, turn, sc2tog, sc in each st to last 2 sts, sc2tog—9 sc.

Row 15: Ch 1, turn, sc in each st across.

Row 16–21: Repeat last 2 rows 3 times—3 sc.

Fold in half, matching up sts of row 1 with row 21. Working through both thicknesses, sl st row 1 and row 21 together. Fasten off, leaving a long tail for sewing.

Assembly

Sew both halves together. Wrap yarn around center about 30 times, stitch through wraps to hold in place.

Edging

Rnd 1: Working in row ends, join A with sc in first row, sc in each row. Repeat for each bow section.

Neckband

With A, ch 4.

Row 1: Sc in 2nd ch from hook and each ch across—3 sc.

Row 2: Ch 1, turn, sc in each st across.

Repeat Row 2 until neckband measures about 12 in. (30.5 cm) long.

Edging

Row 1: Ch 1, working in row ends, sl st in each row.

Fasten off. Repeat across other edge of neckband.

Finishing

With sewing needle and matching thread, sew half of snap to each end of neckband. Sew bow to center of neckband. Weave in ends.

Little Miss Snowball Dress and Hat

SKILL LEVEL

EASY

Red and white are an excellent color combination for any holiday event. When she wears this beautiful dress, your precious baby girl will outshine the holiday lights. It's trimmed at the hem, collar, and cuffs with a furry yarn to keep your little darling toasty warm at all your holiday events.

YARN
Lion Brand Vanna's Glamour (96% Acrylic, 4% Metallic
Polyester; 1.75 oz/50 g; 202 yd./185 m)
#114 Red Stone (A): 3 balls
Lion Brand Fun Fur (100% Polyester; 1.75 oz/50 g;
64 yd./58 m)
#100 White (B): 3 balls

CROCHET HOOKS
U.S. size F-5 (3.75 mm) or size needed to obtain gauge
U.S. size H-8 (5 mm) or size needed to obtain gauge
Note: Use smaller hook throughout unless instructed
otherwise.

ADDITIONAL MATERIALS
Yarn needle

SIZES
3 (6, 9, 12) months
Note: Instructions are given for smallest size; changes for
larger sizes are given in parentheses.

FINISHED MEASUREMENTS
Chest: 17 (18, 18½, 19) in. [43 (45.5, 47, 48.5) cm]
Length: 12½ (14, 14¾, 15¾) in. [32 (35.5, 37.5, 40) cm],
not including hem
Hat Circumference: 16 in. (40.5 cm)

GAUGE
18 sc and 20 rows = 4 in. (10 cm) with smaller hook and A
5 pattern repeats and 13 rnds in lace pattern = 4½ in. (11.5
cm) with smaller hook and A
Note: One pattern repeat consists of one V-st and the
following sc.
10 dc and 6 rnds = 4 in. (10 cm) worked with larger hook and
2 strands of B held together

SPECIAL STITCHES
Single crochet 3 stitches together (sc3tog): [Insert
hook in next stitch, yarn over and draw up a loop]
3 times, yarn over and draw through all 4 loops
on hook.
Shell: 3 dc in same st.
V stitch (V-st): (Dc, ch 2, dc) in same st.

GIRL

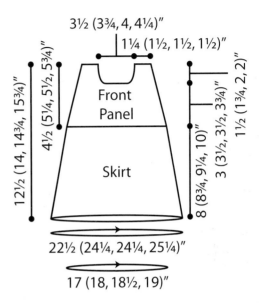

Note: Sleeves are worked directly into
armholes after shoulders are seamed.

DRESS
Bodice Panel (make 2)
With A, ch 39 (42, 43, 44).
Row 1 (RS): Sc in 2nd ch from hook and each ch across—
38 (41, 42, 43) sc.
Rows 2–6: Ch 1, turn, sc2tog, sc in each st to last 2 sts,
sc2tog—28 (31, 32, 33) sc.
Rows 7–15 (17, 18, 19): Ch 1, turn, sc in each st across.

First Shoulder

Row 1: Ch 1, turn, sc in first 9 (10, 10, 10) sts, leaving rem sts unworked—9 (10, 10, 10) sc.

Row 2: Ch 1, turn, sc2tog, sc in each st across—8 (9, 9, 9) sc.

Row 3: Ch 1, turn, sc in each st up to last 2 sts, sc2tog—7 (8, 8, 8) sc.

Row 4: Repeat Row 2—6 (7, 7, 7) sc.

Rows 5–8 (9, 10, 10): Ch 1, turn, sc in each st across. Fasten off after last row.

Second Shoulder

Row 1: Sk next 10 (11, 12, 13) unworked sts after first shoulder and join A with sc in next st, sc in each st across—9 (10, 10, 10) sc.

Row 2: Ch 1, turn, sc in each st up to last 2 sts, sc2tog—8 (9, 9, 9) sc.

Row 3: Ch 1, turn, sc2tog, sc in each st across—7 (8, 8, 8) sc.

Row 4: Repeat Row 2—6 (7, 7, 7) sc.

Rows 5–8 (9, 10, 10): Ch 1, turn, sc in each st across. Fasten off.

Matching up sts of shoulders on front with shoulders on back, sew shoulder seams together.

Neck Shaping

Rnd 1: With RS facing, join A with sc in first skipped st at top of front or back bodice panel, sc in each st across; working over post of sts at row end of shoulder, sc in each row, sc in each skipped st across second bodice panel, sc in each row end of second shoulder, join with sl st in beg sc.

Rnd 2: Ch 1, loosely sl st in each st around. Fasten off.

Collar

Rnd 1: With RS facing and larger hook, working over sl sts of previous rnd, join B with sc in any st of Rnd 1, ch 5, sc in same st, (sc, ch 5, sc) in next st and each st around. Fasten off.

Sleeves (make 2)

Rnd 1: With RS facing and working over posts of sts around armhole opening, join A with sc in Row 1 on front or back bodice panel; sc in next 0 (1, 1, 0) row(s), (sc2tog) 5 (6, 5, 6) times, [shell in next row, sk next row, sc in next row, sk next row] 3 (3, 4, 4) times, shell in center of shoulder seam, [sk next row, sc in next row, sk next row, shell in next row] 3 (3, 4, 4) times, (sc2tog) 5 (6, 5, 6) times, sc in last 1 (2, 2, 1) rows, join with sl st in beg sc—18 (22, 22, 22) sc and 7 (7, 9, 9) shells.

Rnd 2: Ch 1, sc in first 6 (8, 7, 7) sts, sk next st, sc in center st of next shell, [V-st in next sc, sc in center st of next shell] 6 (6, 8, 8) times, sc in next sc and in each st to end, join with sl st in beg sc.

Rnd 3: Ch 1, sc in first 2 (0, 1, 1) st(s), (sc2tog) 2 (4, 3, 3) times, shell in next sc, [sc in next ch-2 sp, shell in next sc] 6 (6, 8, 8) times, (sc2tog) 2 (4, 3, 3) times, sc in last 2 (0, 1, 1) st(s), join with sl st in beg sc—14 (14, 16, 16) sc and 7 (7, 9, 9) shells.

Rnd 4: Ch 1, sc in first 4 sts, sc in center st of next shell, [V-st in next sc, sc in center st of next shell] 6 (6, 8, 8) times, sc in next sc and each st to end, join with sl st in beg sc.

Rnd 5: Ch 1, (sc2tog) twice, shell in next sc, [sc in next ch-2 sp, shell in next sc] 6 (6, 8, 8) times, (sc2tog) twice, join with sl st in beg sc—10 (10, 12, 12) sc and 7 (7, 9, 9) shells.

Rnd 6: Ch 1, sc in first 2 sts, sc in center st of next shell, [V-st in next sc, sc in center st of next shell] 6 (6, 8, 8) times, sc2tog, join with sl st in beg sc—10 (10, 12, 12) sc and 6 (6, 8, 8) V-sts.

Rnd 7: Ch 1, sc in first sc, sk next sc, shell in next sc, [sc in next ch-2 sp, shell in next sc] 6 (6, 8, 8) times, sk last sc, join with sl st in beg sc—7 (7, 9, 9) sc and 7 (7, 9, 9) shells.

Rnd 8: Ch 5 (counts as dc, ch 2 throughout), dc in same st as joining, sc in center st of next shell, [V-st in next sc, sc in center st of next shell] 6 (6, 8, 8) times, join with sl st in 3rd ch of beg ch-5.

Rnd 9: (Sl st, ch 1, sc) in first ch-2 sp, shell in next sc, [sc in next ch-2 sp, shell in next sc] 6 (6, 8, 8) times, join with sl st in beg sc.

Rnds 10–17 (19, 19, 21): Repeat last 2 rnds 4 (5, 5, 6) times.

Rnd 18 (20, 20, 22): Ch 1, sc in first 5 (5, 1, 1) st(s), sc3tog, *sc in next st, sc3tog; repeat from * around, join with sl st in beg sc—16 (16, 18, 18) sc. Fasten off.

Cuffs

Rnd 1: With RS facing and larger hook, join B with sc in any st, ch 5, sc in same st, (sc, ch 5, sc) in next st and each st around. Fasten off.

Skirt

Rnd 1: With RS facing and working in bottom loops of row 1 on either panel, join A with sc in first st, 0 (1, 0, 1) more sc in same st, sc in each st across, working in bottom loops of second panel, 1 (2, 1, 2) sc in first st, sc in each st across, join with sl st in beg sc on first panel—76 (84, 84, 88) sc.

Rnd 2: Ch 1, sc in first st, sk next st, shell in next st, sk next st, *sc in next st, sk next st, shell in next st, sk next st; repeat from * around, join with sl st in beg sc—19 (21, 21, 22) shells.

Rnd 3: Ch 5, dc in same st as join-ing, sc in center st of next shell, *V-st in next sc, sc in center st of next shell; repeat from * around, join with sl st in 3rd ch of beg ch-5—19 (21, 21, 22) V-sts.

Rnd 4: (Sl st, ch 1, sc) in next ch-2 sp, shell in next sc, *sc in next ch-2 sp, shell in next sc; repeat from * around, join with sl st in beg sc.

Rnds 5–6: Repeat Rnds 3–4.

Rnd 7: Ch 5, (dc, ch 2, V-st) in same st as joining, sc in center st of next shell, [V-st in next sc, sc in center st of next shell] 9 (10, 10, 10) times, (V-st, ch 2, V-st) in next sc, place marker in center ch-2 sp, sc in center st of next shell, *V-st in next sc, sc in center st of next shell; repeat from * around, join with sl st in 3rd ch of beg ch-5.

Rnd 8: (Sl st, ch 1, sc) in next ch-2 sp, shell in next ch-2 sp, sc in next ch-2 sp, *shell in next sc, sc in next ch-2 sp; repeat from * to st marker, shell in next (marked) ch-2 sp, move marker to center st of shell just made, sc in next ch-2 sp, shell in next sc, **sc in next ch-2 sp, shell in next sc; repeat from ** around, join with sl st in beg sc—21 (23, 23, 24) shells.

Rnds 9–12: Repeat Rnds 3–4 twice.

Rnd 13: Ch 5, (dc, ch 2, V-st) in same st as joining, sc in center st of next shell, *V-st in next sc, sc in center st of next shell; repeat from * to sc before marked shell, (V-st, ch 2, V-st) in next sc, move marker to center ch-2 sp, sc in center st of next shell, **V-st in next sc, sc in center st of next shell; repeat from ** around, join with sl st in 3rd ch of beg ch-5.

Rnd 14: Repeat Rnd 8—23 (25, 25, 26) shells.

Rnds 15–16 (18, 20, 22): Repeat Rnds 3–4, 1 (2, 3, 4) times.

Rnds 17–18 (19–20, 21–22, 23–24): Repeat Rnds 7–8—25 (27, 27, 28) shells.

Rnds 19–22 (21–24, 23–26, 25–28): Repeat Rnds 3–4 twice.

Rnd 23 (25, 27, 29): Repeat Rnd 3.

Fasten off.

Hem

Rnd 1: With RS facing and larger hook, join B with sc in any ch-2 sp, ch 5, sc in same ch-2 sp, (sc, [ch 5, sc] 3 times) in next sc, *(sc, ch 5, sc) in next ch-2 sp, (sc, [ch 3, sc] 3 times) in next sc; repeat from * around. Fasten off.

Finishing

Weave in ends.

HAT

Holding 2 strands of B together as one, ch 4.

Rnd 1: 9 dc in 4th ch from hook (first 3 chs count as first dc), join with sl st in top of beg ch—10 dc.

Rnd 2: Ch 3, dc in same st, 2 dc in each st around, join with sl st in top of beg ch—20 dc.

Rnd 3: Ch 3, dc in same st, dc in next st, *2 dc in next st, dc in next st; repeat from * around, join with sl st in beg sc—30 dc.

Rnd 4: Ch 3, dc in same st, dc in next 2 sts, *2 dc in next st, dc in next 2 sts; repeat from * around, join with sl st in beg sc—40 dc.

Rnds 5–9: Ch 3, dc in each st around, join with sl st in beg sc.

Rnd 10: Ch 1, sc in first st and in each st around, join with sl st in beg sc. Fasten off.

Finishing

Weave in ends.

Acknowledgments

I am so grateful to all the people that contributed to this venture in one form or another and made this incredible book possible.

All of the fabulous yarns used in this book were generously donated. I am so thankful for each and every one of you: Berroco Inc., Cascade Yarns, Coats and Clark, Elann, Garnstudio DROPS, Lion Brand Yarn, Plymouth Yarn, Tahki Stacy Charles, WEBS, Yarnspirations.

Many thanks also to:

All the adorable babies (and their parents):
Abigail Pope
Caleb Smith
Joseph Ray
Willow Hildebrand

Rachel Greiser, for your wonderful photography and your ability to capture the special moments.

Lisa Johnson, for your incredible styling, insight, patience, and knowing what I need before I do.

My mother Darlene and my stepfather Tony, for allowing us to use your beautiful home and yard for our photo shoots.

Ruth McCandless, for the use of your lovely flower gardens.

Amy Shelton, for your whimsical copywriting.

Angelica Soto, for your flawless model stitching.

Kj Hay, for your impeccable technical editing.

Andrea Graciarena for your wonderful technical editing assistance.

The Crochet Guild of America, for playing such a large role in my path to success.

The "Musketeers": Vashti Braha, Doris Chan, Marty Miller, Diane Moyer. We have come so far since that conference so many years ago!

I would like to thank everyone at Stackpole Books, especially Mark Allison and Kathryn Fulton. I truly appreciate your faith in me and my vision. You have been a joy to work with.

I would also like to thank you, my readers! Without your enthusiasm for my designs I wouldn't be able to do what I do. I am very grateful for your support.

I am so thankful for my fabulous family that I always sorely neglect while working on books: George, my wonderful husband; Chelsea and Shelby, my beautiful daughters; and Willow, my perfect granddaughter.

As always, my greatest gratitude goes to God for this amazing talent He has given me and the opportunities He has presented in my life. I am very blessed.

Yarn and Suppliers

There are many wonderful yarn makers out there; these are just the ones who made the beautiful yarns featured in this book. The specific yarn or yarns used are given in italics for each manufacturer. You can find most of these yarns at your local yarn shop or craft supply store; others can be purchased online.

Berroco, Inc.
Comfort DK; Weekend DK
1 Tupperware Dr., Suite 4
N. Smithfield, RI 02896
(401) 769-1212
http://www.berroco.com

Cascade Yarns
Fixation
Seattle, WA
http://cascadeyarn.com

Coats and Clark
Red Heart Anne Geddes Baby; Red Heart With Love
P.O. Box 12229
Greenville, SC 29612
(800) 648-1479
http://www.coatsandclark.com

Elann
Elann Collection Peruvian Baby Cashmere
P.O. Box 1018
Point Roberts, WA 98281
(604) 952-4096
http://www.elann.com

Garnstudio DROPS
DROPS Cotton Light
(Distributed by Nordic Mart)
http://www.garnstudio.com
http://www.nordicmart.com

Lion Brand Yarn
Fun Fur; Vanna's Glamour Yarn
135 Kero Rd.
Carlstadt, NJ 07072
(800) 258-9276
http://www.lionbrand.com

Plymouth Yarn Company, Inc.
Cleo
500 Lafayette St.
Bristol, PA 19007
(215) 788-0459
http://www.plymouthyarn.com/

Tahki Stacy Charles, Inc.
Cotton Classic
70-60 83rd St., Building #12
Glendale, NY 11385
(718) 326-4433
http://tahkistacycharles.com

WEBS—America's Yarn Store

Valley Yarns Colrain

6 Industrial Pkwy.

Easthampton, MA 01027

(800) 367-9327

http://www.yarn.com/

Yarnspirations.com Headquarters

Caron Simply Soft

320 Livingstone Ave. South

Box 40

Listowel, ON

Canada

N4W 3H3

(888) 368-8401

http://www.yarnspirations.com/

Abbreviations

beg	begin/beginning		**oz**	ounce(s)
BLO	back loops only		**prev**	previous
BPhdc	back post half double crochet		**rem**	remaining
CC	contrasting color		**rnd(s)**	round(s)
ch	chain		**RS**	right side
ch-sp	chain space		**sc**	single crochet
cl	cluster		**sc2tog**	single crochet 2 stitches together
cm	centimeter(s)		**sc3tog**	single crochet 3 stitches together
dc	double crochet		**sk**	skip
dc2tog	double crochet 2 stitches together		**sl st**	slip stitch
FLO	front loops only		**sp(s)**	space(s)
FPdc	front post double crochet		**st(s)**	stitch(es)
FPhdc	front post half double crochet		**tog**	together
FPsc	front post single crochet		**tr**	treble crochet
FPtr	front post treble crochet		**V-st**	V stitch
fsc	foundation single crochet		**WS**	wrong side
g	gram(s)		**yd.**	yard(s)
hdc	half double crochet		**yo**	yarn over
in.	inch(es)		*	repeat instructions following asterisk as directed
lp(s)	loop(s)		( )	work stitches in same st or sp
m	meter(s)		[ ]	work bracketed instructions specified number of times
MC	main color			
mm	millimeter(s)			

Visual Index

Traditional Blessings Christening Gown 2

My Heart Is Yours Boy Cardigan Set 14

Heirloom Blessings Christening Gown 6

Queen of Hearts Girl Cardigan Set 19

Yankee Doodle Dandy Boy Romper and Hat **58**

Sweet as a Daisy Girl Top and Bonnet **73**

Lady Liberty Girl Dress and Hat **63**

Game Changer Boy Jersey, Hat, and Booties **78**

Goldenrod Tank and Hat **70**

Varsity Cheerleader Girl Dress and Headband **83**